HISTORY OF EASTHAMPTON:

ITS SETTLEMENT AND GROWTH;

ITS MATERIAL, EDUCATIONAL, AND RELIGIOUS INTERESTS,

TOGETHER WITH A

Genealogical Record of its Original Families.

By PAYSON W. LYMAN.

NORTHAMPTON:
TRUMBULL & GERE.
1866.

PREFATORY NOTE.

To write the history of one's native town would be a work of peculiar interest to any loyal son. And yet it is a work requiring more research than the limited field would lead one at first thought to suppose. The examination of early town records and manuscripts, and the collection of material which has never been written or recorded, upon various subjects, and from more various sources, has been attended with no little difficulty.

It was to our advantage to have entered, in some degree, into the labors of earlier historians; but their work, though ably performed, did not cover a field so comprehensive as our own. In regard to the settlement and early history of Town and Church, we are glad to acknowledge our large indebtedness to the Semi-Centennial Sermon of Rev. Payson Williston, and to the Historical Sketch of the town, prepared by Rev. Luther Wright, as well as to the researches of the late Sylvester Judd, Esq. The papers of the late Ezekiel White, to which the author was kindly allowed access, were of essential service to him in the preparation of the Genealogical Register, while, concerning dates and events which have occurred during the last half century, no source of information has been so prolific as the memory of his father, Daniel F. Lyman.

While we thus acknowledge our indebtedness to these, we desire to tender our sincerest thanks to the many others, who, in one way or another, have rendered us aid.

Where our plan has led us to speak of individuals, particularly in the Genealogical Register, our estimate of character, in cases of men to whom our memory does not extend, has been based upon the judgment of others. Because we have in some instances spoken in commendatory terms of certain persons, it should not therefore be inferred that they were the only good and worthy men, or indeed perhaps, the best. We have judged it advisable, even at the risk of some charge of unfairness, to relieve the tedium of a bare recital of the facts ordinarily detailed in a genealogical record, by the narration of incidents, bits of personal history, and the occasional mention of prominent characteristics.

We desire to bespeak for this sketch, freedom from harsh criticism and hasty judgment. We do not claim for it infallibility, but entertain the hope that it will be found essentially correct.

Such as it is, we send it forth in the hope that it may contribute its share to the maintenance of a firm attachment to the institutions of our fathers, from an appreciation of their worth, and to the perpetuation of the names of those who founded and those who have thus far built up the town, as well as of those who have upheld its honor, and that of the nation, on the varied fields of conflict and toil to which the providence of God has called them.

P. W. L.

EASTHAMPTON, October, 1866.

CONTENTS.

CHAPTER VIII.

CHAPTER IX.

CHAPTER X.

HISTORY OF EASTHAMPTON.

CHAPTER I.

SETTLEMENT.—EARLY HISTORY.

THIS thriving town is beautifully situated. It is such a spot as a lover of nature might select for a residence. Its streams, flowing down from the mountains which encircle it, bearing fertility on their bosoms, the mountains themselves standing like watch-towers guarding it, its variation of hill and dale and plain, its beautiful trees and streets, all combine to render it a delightful retreat from the cares and turmoils of city life. Its steeples, educational institutions, factories, and well-cultivated farms, tell that it is inhabited by an intelligent, enterprising, and industrious people, and that here education and religion have not been forgotten.

The town was settled by a race of sober, industrious men, who instilled into the minds of their children the great truths of the Bible, who frowned upon vice wherever seen, who sought not popularity and ease, who endeavored to walk in the path of duty, and as a consequence, vice and crime have never flourished within its limits. The sterner virtues here found a strong foothold. Cradled in the lap of agriculture, inured to toil, privation and danger, they and their children grew up a hardy, healthy people.

That they loved the Bible and sanctuary, and that they reverenced the Sabbath, is seen in the sacrifices they willingly made to attend the stated preaching of the Word. Before any church was built here, they went to Northampton or Southampton every Sabbath, unless something extraordinary prevented. They did not, as is becoming somewhat fashionable, go to meeting in the forenoon and stay at home in the afternoon. Neither were they wearied with a sermon of an hour's length. That they did not consult ease, we may conclude from the fact that all, old and young, male and female, could rise and stand while God's blessing was being invoked. If any one sat during the prayer, it was justly concluded that they were sick or infirm. If, on a particular Sabbath, any one was noticed to sit, it was not strange if the person were the subject of anxious solicitude during the week. A law once existed subjecting persons to a fine for absenting themselves from public worship for three months. In one or two instances in town, this law was enforced.

Their Sabbath commenced at sunset, or dusk, Saturday night. Before this, in many instances, the father had finished his work and shaved himself, the mother had prepared the food for the next day as far as possible, all work had ceased, and, to quote the language of another, "Both parents, with their children, and the book of God open before them, were often waiting ere the setting of the sun to cross together the sacred threshold of the Sabbath." Would that their children of the present day had more regard for the sacred day. They were patriotic also. In no town were the inhabitants more universally loyal. Venerable men! It was yours to lay the foundations of society broad and deep, to stamp upon it a respect and love for the institutions of religion, to plant high its standard of morals; and nobly have you fulfilled your mission. Your record is on high; and not only there, but it is seen in the character and reputation your children have held. The influence which you have exerted and do exert through your sons, who are scattered all the way from the Atlantic to the Pacific, from the great lakes to the Gulf of Mexico, will forever endure. It is deathless as the sun; aye, when that luminary himself has faded, it will live on and on.

SETTLEMENT.

Easthampton was originally a part of a tract of land called Nonotuck, signifying "in the midst of the river," embracing the four Hamptons and a part of Montgomery and Hatfield. It was purchased of the Indians in 1653, for one hundred fathoms of wampum, ten coats, plowing sixteen acres of land in *Hadleigh*, and some small gifts. It was a sum small in itself and intrinsically of no great value, but, as they reserved the right of hunting and fishing on them, and as the articles were of great exchangeable value among the Indians, they received ample remuneration for the land. It was conveyed to the settlers by a deed of Chickwallop and six others. It appears that after the purchase, Sachem Umpanchela complained that he had not received his portion of the purchase price. The planters immediately satisfied him. They represented in their petition to the General Court for liberty to settle here, that it was a place suitable to erect a town for the public weal and for the propagation of the Gospel.

Without doubt, John Webb was the first inhabitant of Easthampton. The time and place of his settlement is not quite certain. Previous histories concur in giving him a residence in Nashawannuck, with no definite date. In the town records of Northampton, under date of Dec. 13,

1664, we find that the town granted John Webb a piece of land at Pascommuck, to build a house upon. In February of the same year we find the following:—"I, John Webb, Sen., of Pascommuck, doe engage, &c." He was a citizen of Northampton as early as 1657, for in July of that year we find a deed of land sold to Northampton by Sachem Umpanchela and Lampanoho. They received the pay of "John Webb of Northampton." Whether or not he then resided within the present limits of Easthampton is uncertain. In 1663 or '4 it was recorded by the town clerk that John Webb brought several wolves' heads, probably to receive the bounty offered by the town or colony. He died in 1670. Families by the name of Webb continued to reside in Nashawannuck for more than 75 years. After the death of Mr. Webb, Robert Danks married his widow, and families of this name resided here until after 1760.

The next portion of what is now Easthampton which was settled, was on the north side of the Manhan river, near the present center of the town. Probably the first building erected there was a saw mill, situated near the house of Joel Bassett, on Sawmill Brook. In 1674, the town gave "David Wilton, Medad Pumry and Joseph Taylor liberty to erect a saw-mill on the brook, on the right hand of the cartway going over Manhan river." In 1686–7, Northampton gave Samuel Bartlett liberty to set up a corn-mill "on the falls below the cartway on the river." The mill was doubtless built soon after, but how soon a house was erected and a settlement made is not certainly known, probably not, however, till some years after 1705, owing to the French and Indian war. But this much is certain, that Joseph Bartlett, son of Samuel, made the first permanent settlement here. The mill and land about it was given him by his father in 1705. He kept the first public house in town and had charge of it for more than twenty years.

He died in 1755, leaving most of his property to his relatives, the Clapps, one of whom, Jonathan, afterwards Major, who will be spoken of in the history of the Clapp family, resided with him for some years. He gave some land, however, to three of his brothers, on condition that they should give £100 old tenor, equal in value to £13 6s. 8d. lawful money, to the first church of Christ that should be erected and celebrate divine ordinances within half a mile of his house. This payment was afterwards made with the proceeds of land disposed of at Pogue's Hole. This bequest shows the interest he felt in the institutions of the Gospel, and the hope, very likely the expectation, he cherished, that at some time a church would be organized here.

About the year 1726 or 8, four brothers by the name of Wait, planted themselves near the residence of John Scott. One of them died in 1732, another in 1745, and the other two, after many years, moved away.

David Bartlett, brother of Landlord Joseph, built a a house about forty rods west of where Julius Pomeroy now resides, not far from 1725. He lived and died on the place and left it to his son David, who also occupied it till his death, which occurred just before the American Revolution commenced. To this house, during the war, persons afflicted with that terrible disease, the small pox, (rendered doubly terrible from the fact that nothing had then been discovered to deprive the disease of its virulence,) were taken. Among the number of its inmates was Col. Hosford, who was brought from Northampton. He died here and was buried in a field a little way from the house. Rev. John Hooker, the successor of Rev. Jonathan Edwards, D. D., in the ministry at Northampton, also died at this place. He took the disease by simply passing the house in which Col. Hosford was confined before being removed. His remains were carried by night around through the meadows to the cemetery at Northampton, and there interred. This house was standing till within a few years.

Northampton originally appropriated the meadows, supposed to contain one hundred acres, more or less, eighty acres above and twenty below the grist mill, for the use of schools. For many years they leased it to different individuals, but in 1745 they sold all the upper meadow to Dea. Stephen Wright and Benjamin Lyman. Shortly after they removed here, Benjamin Lyman settled where the house of Joel Bassett stands, and Dea. Wright where Samuel Hurlburt resides.

In 1755, an expedition was planned against Crown Point, and the command entrusted to Sir Wm. Johnson. His army arrived at the south end of Lake George before transporation had been provided. While waiting for batteaux to convey him to Crown Point, he received intelligence that a detachment of French Regulars, Canadians, and Indians, under command of Baron Dieskau, was approaching Fort Edward for the purpose of destroying some provision and military stores. Johnson at once called a council of war, at which it was determined to dispatch Col. E. Williams to intercept the French on their return from the fort. Diskeau, however, changed his course, with the intention of attacking Johnson's camp. Col. Williams was not aware of the change, and he marched on to his doom, apprehensive of no danger. The enemy had been apprised of his approach and lay in ambush for him. The firing commenced prematurely, but was very destructive. The surprise was complete. The brave commander, in endeavoring to conduct his troops to a more advantageous position, received a ball in his head, which instantly killed him. The firing continued with unabated fury, and they were obliged to retreat to the camp, whither they were closely followed by the enemy, who were received by Johnson with a murderous discharge of cannon and musketry, which did so much execution among them that they retired in great disorder, leaving on the field Baron Dieskau, who had received a mortal wound in his thigh. He fell into the hands of the Americans, and said, before his death, that, in all his military life, nothing had ever sent death into his army like the prolonged cheers which the Americans gave at their approach. Each of these neighbors, last referred to, had a son in this battle, which took place Sept. 8, 1775, and in which Col. Ephraim Williams, the generous founder of Williams College, and more than two hundred others were slain, among whom was Sergeant Eliakim Wright, son of Stephen, aged 28. Lemuel Lyman, son of Benjamin, then twenty years of age, was in company with Sergeant Wright, one of the scouting party who was sent out to reconnoitre. They met the enemy advancing in the form of a crescent, but did not discover them until they were partially inclosed, whereupon a warm fire opened. Mr. Lyman was in the act of firing at an Indian, when a ball struck him. It passed across three of his fingers and struck his breast, passing through a leather vest, three thicknesses of his shirt, and his bullet pouch, which was providentially in that place, and half buried itself in his body. The pouch is still preserved in one of the numerous families of his descendants. There were four other soldiers standing near him, three of whom were killed there, and the other one after he reached the camp. Shortly after he obtained a furlough and returned home, laden with news both joyful and sad. The French had been successfully resisted, and repulsed with great loss, but our own army had not escaped unhurt; about forty-six persons belonging to the Hampshire regiment had fallen; a neighbor and friend had been stricken down, and it was his task to break the sad intelligence to the bereaved family. The sorrow was mitigated by the pleasing consciousness that he was prepared to obey the summons, yet it was a severe blow, and one which fell where least expected. From the families of those neighbors, the oldest and most experienced was taken, the youngest spared. When the two were about to depart, Mr. Lyman said to Mr. Wright, "If my son was only as old as yours, I should not feel so much anxiety." After the battle, Mr. Wright reminded him of the conversation, and said, "Now my son is killed, while yours is only wounded."

Soon after, he with several others, collected a small drove of cattle and started with them for the northern army. Being insufficiently supplied with provisions, they suffered exceedingly from hunger on their journey. On one occasion they obtained and cooked a small quantity of meat which was somewhat tainted, but it was their mutual testimony that they never tasted that which was sweeter.

Benjamin Lyman, above mentioned, was the ancestor of all the persons of that name residing in the town. He had four sons and three daughters. Dea. Stephen Wright was the ancestor of all the families in town of that name. He had four sons. The descendants of these two families, many of whom still reside in Easthampton, are widely scattered. Probably they can be found in more than half of the states and territories in the Union. At least nineteen of them have been college graduates.

Not far from the close of the Revolutionary War, Joseph and Titus Wright moved to the south of Rocky

Hill and lived many years near the house now owned and occupied by Dwight Lyman, but they finally left town.

The third settlement in town was commenced in the year 1700, at Pascommuck, by five families, on land now owned by L. W. Parsons, Joseph Parsons, and Gilbert A. Clark. Their names were Moses Hutchinson, who settled farthest west, John Searl, Benoni Jones, Samuel Janes, and Benjamin Janes. In 1704, this village was destroyed by the Indians under circumstances of the most shocking barbarity. A more full account of this massacre will be given in another place. It was not re-settled until about 1715. The new settlers of Pascommuck, after the slaughter, were Nathaniel Alexander, who married the widow of John Searl, (he having been slain by the Indians,) and lived several years on his farm. Samuel Janes, Jr., took the place of his father. In 1720, John Lankton purchased the lot originally owned by Benoni Jones. He lived however, only nine years to enjoy it. His widow married a man by the name of Wharton, but for some cause he soon left her and she was for many years known as Widow Wharton. Her son, John Lankton, afterwards removed to West Springfield. His father owned a slave while he lived in Pascommuck, which was valued at £60 in his inventory. It appears that Joseph Bartlett was also a slaveholder, from the fact that he set two slaves free by his will. There is also a slave mentioned in the list of Major Clapp's estate, but whether it was one that he purchased, or one of those set free by his Uncle Bartlett, (which is not an unlikely supposition,) is not certain. These were doubtless the only cases of slave ownership in town. The place of John Searl was occupied by his son Elisha, after his return from Canada, whither he had been carried by the Indians at the sacking of the village in 1702. Ebenezer Ferry, from Springfield, at a later period, purchased the Hutchinson place and lived on it twenty-five years or more. He died in 1752.

The first settlers in that part of Easthampton which was then Southampton, with the exception of Dea. Stephen Wright, were Samuel and Eldad Pomeroy and their sons, who established themselves near where Dea. E. W. Hannum now resides, it is presumed about 1732. Caleb Pomeroy, son of Samuel, soon after built a house near where A. L. Strong now lives. He died in 1812, leaving two sons, Enos and Solomon. Probably about 1760, John and Eleazar Hannum located themselves on the places which their descendants now occupy. Joel Hannum, a brother of John and Eleazer, lived in Nashawannuck. He had one son, Paul, who lived for a while on the old place. He afterwards removed to Bainbridge, Ohio, where he lived many years. He died Dec. 28, 1861, aged 76.

The first settler on the plain was Sergeant Ebenezer Corse. It is not certain at what time he came there, probably about 1732. He built the house where Spencer Clapp formerly lived, now owned by James Nichols. It is to him that the town is indebted for one of its handsomest streets, (Main Street,) running from the center of the town straight to his house, a distance of more than a mile, he having cleared away the woods for a road. He was a bold, fearless man. It is said of him that he refused to remove to the fort, where the other settlers fled on account of the Indians. But he finally found traces of an ambush which had been laid for him, which convinced him that discretion was the better part of valor, and he accordingly repaired thither for the time being. He died May 4, 1776, two months before the Declaration of Independence, in the 85th year of his age. His wife died eight years before him, in her 73d year. Both were buried in the old cemetery.

He was followed soon after by other settlers, one of whom was Stephen Wright, son of Dea. Stephen, one of the purchasers of School Meadow. He built the house until recently occupied by his grandson, John Wright. Other settlers in this neighborhood were Aaron Clapp, Benjamin Clapp, and Benjamin Lyman, a son of the other purchaser of the meadow.

That part of the west district known as Park Hill, derives its name, it is said, from an inclosure that was built upon it for the purpose of aiding in the capture of deer. As early as 1750, Mr. Josiah Phelps built a house on the site of the recent residence of J. R. Wright. He had no children, and at his death it passed into the hands of Jonathan Bartlett, a son-in-law of his wife. Mr. Phelps was a very good and pious, though somewhat eccentric man. It is said that on one occasion, in speaking of a piece of new land which he had broken up, he said that while he was doing it, his mind was so absorbed with thoughts of himself, his relations to God, and his hopes of Heaven, that he paid no attention to his team.

The first settlement in the south-east part of the town was made by Israel Hendrick, who removed from Connecticut about the year 1774, and built a log house on the east side of Broad Brook, about opposite from where Pearson Hendrick now lives. A few years after he removed a little farther up the brook and built a small framed house. The other early settlers of this district were Joel Robbins, Benjamin Stephens, and Benjamin Strong, who was in the sixth generation from Richard Strong of Taunton, Somersetshire, England. His son, Elder John Strong, came from England to Dorchester in the same company with Capt. Roger Clapp, from whence he removed to Windsor, Ct., in 1635, and from there to Northampton in 1659, where he died April, 1699, aged 94.

INDIAN TROUBLES.

On the 24th of May, 1704, the village of Pascommuck was destroyed by the Indians. It had then been settled only four or five years. A party of Indians, it seems, had been to Merrimac river, for some reason, but not accomplishing their purpose, they directed their course towards Westfield. Westfield river was however so much swollen by the rains, that they could not pass it. Some of this party knew the situation of Pascommuck, and as they had been unable for some time to obtain food, they determined as a last resort, as they afterwards declared, to make a descent upon the village to satisfy their hunger, and as we are compelled to believe by their conduct, to satisfy also their natural ferocity. Accordingly on the evening previous to the attack, they came along on the mountain, in order to examine its situation and fix a plan of attack. It was for them a favorable circumstance that the meadows intervening between the fated settlement and Northampton were overflowed, and all direct land communication with it cut off. On the morning of May 24th, just before daybreak, they descended and commenced an attack, as unexpected on the part of the inhabitants as it was furious and terrible on theirs.

It appears that a defense was attempted at the house of Benoni Jones, which was encompassed with pickets, but the surprise was so complete that the savages, aided by fire, were soon enabled to overpower and destroy, or capture nearly all of them. Nineteen or twenty were slain. Nine persons by the name of Janes were killed:—Samuel, his wife and three children, and four children of Benjamin Janes. The wife of the latter was taken by the savages to the top of Pomeroy mountain, and there knocked on the head and scalped, and probably left for dead. By a good Providence she was not killed, but was found in this situation, and carried on a litter to Northampton. Her husband, after the capture, had fallen a little in rear of the party, and while they were passing a little ravine, surrounded by bushes and leading to the water, near the present residence of Bryant Pendleton, he succeeded in eluding the vigilance of his savage captors. Running through this he reached the water, and springing into a skiff, which he probably knew to be fastened there, he made his escape to Northampton, where he was the first to announce the mournful tidings.

A troop of cavalry, headed by Capt. John Taylor, immediately started to intercept, if possible, the relentless savages. He came through Pomeroy's meadow, near the present road leading from East to Westhampton, and passed on south to the so-called Westfield road, and between this and Mt. Tom, on land now owned by Chester and the heirs of C. Edson Wait, he encountered the Indians. They having by some means obtained knowledge of his approach, destroyed the lives of all the boys whom they had captured, except Elisha, son of John Searl. He, seeing the work of destruction going on, caught a pack and ran on, thereby showing that if they would spare him he would be no hindrance but rather a help to them. Capt. Taylor, being considerably in advance of his troops, was exposed to the first fire of the enemy, who were probably concealed, and fell. It is not known whether any others were killed, but it is certain that the Indians escaped.

Benjamin Janes removed to Coventry, Ct., where he was made deacon of the church. The wife of John Searl survived a severe blow on the head from a tomahawk. One of her descendants has in her possession a silver hair pin worn on the head of Mrs. Searl at the time the blow was inflicted. Her son Elisha, who was not murdered,

2

was taken to Canada, where he was brought up in the Catholic faith, and his mind became thoroughly imbued with its superstitions. On one occasion, with a party of Indians, he made arrangements to enter on a hunting and trapping expedition along the great western lakes, for the purpose of obtaining fur. As no priest was to accompany them, he went to one and inquired, with evident concern, what he should do, since there was no priest to whom he could confess, and he might die on his journey. The priest told him it would be just as well to confess to a tree, and then sent him away. This declaration struck him very forcibly. He revolved the idea in his mind, and the result was that he become convinced that the whole system of Romanism was one of deception, and on his return he refused to confess his sins to a priest. After many years he visited his native place, but so accustomed had he become to Canadian, or Indian life, that it was with the greatest difficulty that his friends prevailed on him to stay. It is said that during his long absence he had so far forgotten the English language, that he was unable to make himself known to his friends, and that he succeeded in doing so only when he had found in the house and walked upon a pair of stilts which he had used when a boy. Here he married, reared up a family, was a worthy citizen, and held a respectable standing in the church. As an instance of the power of early associations upon the mind, it may be mentioned that on one occasion, as he was by the bedside of a dying woman, under the influence, for the moment, of his early delusion, he requested her to remember him in her prayers in Heaven, but instantly recollecting himself, he expressed sorrow that he should ever have made such a request.

No other lives were known to have been taken by the Indians, till 1724, when Nathaniel Edwards, 2d, was shot at the brook a few rods south of the residence of Samuel Phelps. It was supposed that he, in company with other men from Northampton, had come out to gather their crops from the Manhan meadows, which were leased for a long time previous to their purchase. Several of them came out together for the sake of mutual protection, but he, it is said, was detained at the cartway or fording place on the river, in consequence of which he fell behind the others, was waylaid at the above mentioned place, and was shot and scalped, by a body of Indians. The tradition is that there was a negro on the load at the time. His attention being attracted by the firing and shouting, he raised his head and looked cautiously over, when, to his horror and dismay, he beheld the swarthy savages scalping his master. He however remained quiet till the team had reached the top of the hill, when he slipped from the load, removed one horse from the team, mounted, and made off with all possible speed towards Northampton. Before reaching it, he overtook the other teamsters, and informed them of his master's fate. It is not known whether the murderers were pursued, but it is certain that they escaped unpunished.

It is probable that these were the only persons killed by the Indians within what now constitutes Easthampton, but for more than twenty years from this time,—particularly, however, in 1745, 6 and 7,—a general fear of the tenants of the forest pervaded the community; so much so, that about 1745 several houses were fortified, as places of refuge in case of an attack, and mounts were erected as watch-houses. The houses of Joseph Bartlett at the Mills, Samuel Janes at Pascommuck, and Major Clapp near where Ansel Bartlett now resides, were thus guarded.

Those were times of peculiar danger, and it is well that we, their children, should remember at what price of blood, treasure, and comfort, our homes and our liberties, both civil and religious, were obtained, in order that we may the more sacredly guard them; that we may be the more anxious to transmit them, unimpaired, to those that shall come after us.

As we have seen, these grounds which we now call our own, were once the home of the red man. Here they roamed in savage freedom, built their wigwams, sang their war songs, and celebrated the exploits of their sires. They enjoyed peculiar facilities for fishing, for the falls on Manhan river, by the grist-mill, afforded facilities which all did not enjoy. There is abundant testimony that shad and salmon in large quantities were taken there. These plains were the resort of large numbers of deer, which afforded them means of subsistence, as well as suited their natural tastes and desires. The last place in town which they occupied, was in the limits of Pascommuck, where they had a village and a fort, probably on what is now known as Fort Plain, in the rear of the East District school-house.

In 1664, a number of them petitioned the town of Northampton for liberty to erect a fort. The town granted the petition on seven conditions, the first being that they should not violate the Sabbath, by carrying burdens, or in any other manner. The other restrictions were concerning harboring other Indians, &c. Their motives were probably good in desiring the place. They had no evil designs against the dominant race. They continued to reside here, till the opening of King Phillip's war, in 1675, when they joined the hostile forces, and quitted forever the land of their nativity—the home of their fathers.

Perhaps we can imagine, better than describe, their feelings, when they surveyed, for the last time, the hills, valleys and rivers,—the theaters of their brave exploits, immortalized in song.

There is much to admire, as well as much to deprecate, in their character. That they had vices none can question. That they had virtues, is equally true. But they are gone; not an individual left. The race which once roamed these hillsides, hunted deer in these grand old forests, and fished in these streams, are remembered only in history. They passed away, so far as we know, unblessed by the gospel, which alone maketh wise unto salvation.

There is not now much to remind us of that once interesting though fearful people; but what there is should be preserved and perpetuated.

Two portions of the town still retain the old Indian names to some extent. I refer to Pascommuck and Nashawannuck. Surely these are names of which no son or daughter of these places, or of Easthampton, need be ashamed. The latter of these names, it hardly need be said, has been adopted by one manufacturing company in town. It is well. Let these names forever remain, sad mementoes of the departed, almost forgotten, race. Let them descend to the latest generation.

We have now reviewed, somewhat at length, the settlement of the different portions of the town. We have seen that some of the settlers had to encounter perils from the wild, merciless savage, whom they had reason to fear by day and night; or, if the red man did not disturb their homes, there were forests to be felled before farming lands could be obtained, houses to be constructed, roads to be built, and all this with utensils which appear rude indeed when compared with those of modern times. But all these hardships were, no doubt, intended by an All-wise Providence for the development of that sterling type of character, which has so long been the glory and boast of our loved New England.

INCORPORATION.

The first attempt, on the part of the inhabitants of Easthampton, to become a town or district, was in March, 1773. At that time, what is now Easthampton, belonged to Northampton and Southampton. It was divided as follows:—"All east of a line beginning near the bridge over the Manhan river, and running southwardly on the Westfield road, so-called, to land owned by the late Gamaliel Pomeroy, in Southampton; and all northwardly of a line commencing near the mouth of Sawmill Brook, and extending westwardly in the rear of the houses now owned by Samuel Hurlburt and Samuel Wright, to the road just beyond S. Wright's house, along said road westwardly through the house now owned by Dea. E. W. Hannum, towards Pomeroy mountain. All east and north of these lines belonged to Northampton; the rest of course to Southampton." The motives which actuated our fathers in pressing a separation, were that they might be in such circumstances, that, with little difficulty, they could meet and transact business among themselves; but more especially, that, with greater convenience, and hopefully with greater profit to themselves and their families, they might attend on public worship and ordinances of God's sanctuary. Laudable and praiseworthy motives, truly! In accordance with these views, in 1773 they requested the inhabitants of Northampton and Southampton to consider the subject and report.

The former chose a committee, who reported in favor of the petition, and proposed the lines for the new town, and advocated the raising of £300, to aid them in erecting a meeting house and settling a minister. The town accepted the report of the committee, and subsequently directed their representative to use his influence in the General

Court in favor of the petition; but the project met with strong opposition from Southampton, and the revolutionary war came on, so that it was delayed for some years. In 1781-2 the subject was again agitated. Northampton again voted to set off the new town. Estimating those who would be set off, at one-eighth of the inhabitants of the town, they proposed to give them one-eighth of all the public property of the town, and something more; but the district was not incorporated, owing, it is presumed, to the opposition of Southampton, till 1785.

In the summer of that year, the act incorporating Easthampton as a district, passed the legislature, and Robert Breck, Esq., was empowered to issue his warrant, directed to one of the principal inhabitants, directing him to warn the citizens to assemble for the choice of officers. His warrant was directed to Benjamin Lyman. The first district meeting was held at the house of Capt. Joseph Clapp.

The question may arise in some minds, "Why was it not incorporated as a town?" In answer to this, Dr. Holland says:—"Before 1753, the governor of Massachusetts received instructions from the home government, which, in a strong light, exhibited the growing jealousy of the crown, of the popular element in the government of the colony. The increase in the number of towns in the colony, increasing in the same ratio the representation in the legislature, was seen to present formidable encroachments upon the authority of the parent power. To put a stop to this, the governor was instructed to consent to no act for establishing a new town, with the right of representation, for many years; as a substitute, districts were incorporated, with the full privileges of towns, except representation."

This, of course, was previous to the revolutionary war,

but after the nation had become independent, it seems that the practice was continued for a limited time.

The number of families set off from Northampton, was probably less than 60, and the number of persons not far from 300. These, with those set off from Southampton, made the population of the district a few more than 400 souls.

The lines of separation between this and the other towns, was somewhat irregular. It was to some extent a matter of choice with many of the borderers, whether they would belong to Easthampton, or not. Several families, who *ought* to have belonged, and who, otherwise, *would* have belonged to Easthampton, were, by order of the legislature, allowed to remain citizens of North or Southampton. This gave rise to great irregularity in the town lines, which may be seen at a glance on any county map.

CHAPTER II.

CHURCHES.

In 1781–2, so strong was belief of the people that they should soon become a district and corporate society, that they made preparations to erect a suitable place of public worship. At length, in the spring of 1785, a frame, "of suitable size, and good materials," was erected, on the responsibility, as it appears, of individuals. On the 13th of July, at the first business meeting of the district, they voted to provide a place for public worship, and also to make use of the frame already erected, which stood on the land now enclosed for a park, near the present location of the First Church. They also voted to remunerate those who had erected the frame, in the summer of that same year. It was clap-boarded, shingled, and the lower floor laid, but was not entirely finished till 1792. The building was 53 feet long, and 42 feet wide, with neither bell nor steeple, but was a well finished house. Of this building, Rev. Mr. Williston, in a semi-centennial sermon, preached August 18, 1839, from 2 Peter, 1, 12: says:— "For a little more than fifty years was this house the place of our holy solemnities. Thither were the fathers and mothers in our Israel, till successively removed by death, seen to be resorting almost as constantly as the Sabbath returned. And there, with many sustaining the relations of children and grand-children to them, and I may add, with others also, it was their delight to meet, and together to pray and praise, and to think and talk of heaven."

The first church was organized Nov. 17, 1785, at the house of Capt. Joseph Clapp. It consisted of seventy-two members, forty-six of whom had been dismissed from the church in Northampton, twenty-six from the church in Southampton. They made choice of Mr. Stephen Wright for Moderator, and Philip Clark for Clerk. In 1786, Benjamin Lyman, Stephen Wright and Philip Clark, were appointed to collect the donation of Joseph Bartlett, to the first church of Christ which should be organized and celebrate divine ordinances within half a mile of his house. It, together with the interest accruing thereon, amounted to £14 1s 3d, and was expended in the purchase of a communion service. In the same year, the district hired Rev. Aaron Walworth to preach. They afterward gave a call to him to setttle with them as their pastor, but he saw fit to decline the invitation.

On the 6th of April, 1789, they gave Rev. Payson Williston a call to settle in the gospel ministry, and agreed to give him a settlement fund of £180, and a salary of £65 the first year, to be increased twenty shillings a year, until it amounted to £70, besides thirty-five cords of wood per year, "if he shall need so much for his own consumption."

Mr. Williston accepted the call, and was ordained Aug. 13, 1789. The services were conducted as follows:—Introductory prayer by Rev. Enoch Hale of Westhampton; Sermon by Rev. Noah Williston; Consecrating Prayer by Rev. Richard S. Storrs; Concluding Prayer by Rev. Seth Payson. Previous to his ordination, the church observed a day of fasting and prayer, in accordance with a fitting custom of those days.

The first deacons of the church were Stephen Wright and Benjamin Lyman, chosen in 1786.

At the commencement of his ministry in Easthampton, Mr. Williston was twenty-six years of age. About the time of his settlement, on one occasion, when the militia company, including all who were sixteen years of age, were assembled for exercise, it was proposed that they should signify whether the candidate was one of their choice. The result was entire unanimity in his favor.

In the past history of Easthampton, no man has occupied a position so prominent and influential, for so long a time, as the first pastor of the church, and this fact may justify a notice of him somewhat more extended than would otherwise be given. Many of the facts and statements are derived from the sermon preached at his funeral by Rev. John Woodbridge, D. D., then pastor in Hadley.

Rev. Payson Williston was born in West Haven, Ct., in 1763, and was the son of the Rev. Noah Williston of that place. His mother was of the family of Payson, who were connected with the well-known ministers of that name. His religious training was blessed by his early conversion. He decided to enter the ministry, and studied under the instruction of the excellent Dr. Trumbull of North Haven, Conn. He entered Yale College in 1778 or 1779, and graduated in 1783. "He numbered among his classmates men distinguished in professional and literary life, among whom were the Rev. Dr. Morse, the geographer, Rev. Dr. Holmes, Hon. J. C. Smith, since governor of Conn., and the Hon. David Daggett, well known for his legal attainments, and as an able jurist." Before entering college he was engaged for several months in the service of his country, in the war of the Revolution, and knew by experience the dangers and difficulties which our fathers encountered, in the struggle for freedom and independence; and for several years before his death, he received a pension for the service performed in that struggle. He was licensed to preach at twenty-one, but did not choose to settle till he had gained some experience in the ministerial life. After preaching for several years in vacant parishes, he accepted the call of the church in this place, and became its first pastor. In 1790 he married Miss Sarah Birdseye, daughter of Rev. Nathan Birdseye, of Stratford, Ct. "With this amiable wife of his youth, whose sound sense, industry, and prudence rendered her a great blessing to her family, he lived happily for nearly fifty-five years. She passed away in the year 1845, at the age of 82."

In 1805, Mr. Williston, without being dismissed from his charge, was employed as a missionary, in the frontier and sparsely populated settlements in Western New York, where is now the very center of abundance, agricultural cultivation, and advancement in the necessary and elegant arts of life. For forty-four years he faithfully and cheerfully performed the duties incumbent upon him, as an embassador of the Cross, and for more than sixty years, he was, as pastor, adviser, and neighbor, instrumental of great good to his people. His doctrinal views were much like those of our Puritan Fathers. He preached with plainness, but with variety, and fullness of illustration, and not unfrequently with much emotion. His example afforded the most beautiful enforcement and exemplification of his doctrine. His life was a preaching life, till it terminated in the silence of death. Modesty was one of his most prominent characteristics. He was never obtrusive; and as for boasting, one who knew him well said: "we should almost as soon have expected to see a violation of the laws of nature, as to hear a word of this kind from the lips of Mr. Williston." But having arrived at the age of seventy, though still in the enjoyment of the fullest confidence and esteem of his people, he judged it expedient to withdraw from the active duties of the ministry. Accordingly, at a meeting of the town, March 11, 1833, in their corporate capacity, including the brethren of the church, he presented the following communication:

"*Men and Brethren:*—It has been my purpose for years, should I attain to the period of life I have, and at the same time be sustaining the relation of pastor to you, to manifest a willingness to have a colleague settled with me—or, should you deem it preferable, to relinquish my ministry among you, when you shall have become united in some one to be my successor, and he shall be placed over you in the Lord—or indeed earlier, if it should appear generally best that I should. Sooner much than I anticipated, have I entered upon my seventieth year; and though, at present, I am freer from bodily pains and infirmities, than is ordinarily the case with persons of my standing, my age teacheth me that my working time must ere long be over, and that, while it continues, I may be losing my ability for performing the service you need—or, to be sure, all you may think,—or, in fact may be desirable. I should exceedingly regret being in the way of any one, upon whose ministrations you can hope to attend, with the rational prospect of greater advantage to your souls, than can be looked for, by a much longer attendance on mine. Your interests, especially your immortal, I trust, I have never regarded with indifference, or ever shall; and though in my ministry, I see I have not had all that concern on my mind for your temporal and spiritual advantage and welfare, which has been my duty, and have not, as an humble instrument in the hands of the Lord, been active and engaged for the promotion of the one and the other, to the extent your circumstances required, yet I do hope, that I have not altogether labored in vain, and that the results have been happy to no inconsiderable numbers, and will appear so in eternity. For the many years I have been attempting to instruct, and in this place, guide souls to heaven, my ministry has been attended with less to perplex, and more to tranquilize the mind, than usually has fallen to the lot of my fellow laborers. And here I am constrained to say, (and I do it with pleasure,) that, under God, I consider this is very much owing to the respect shown by those active in my settlement,—mostly now in their graves,—and generally by their children, to the Sabbath and the institutions of religion, and, with reference to my usefulness and comfort, their frequently and promptly making me some consideration, when the support they had voted me was found to be inadequate. The support, however, I have received, has never been such as to render desirable anything farther being done. My means for living are probably considerably less than numbers of you are apprehensive; and should my pastoral relation to you soon be dissolved, in any other way than by death, you will see, that at least, some consideration may be needful for me the little time that may still be allotted me to live; and as I was settled for life, I have a pleasing confidence that it will be granted. How much, or how little, I do not take upon myself to say. The subject is a delicate one, and I am willing to leave it to your love of justice and generosity to determine. I feel grateful to you, my friends, under Providence, that my youth, the meridian of my life, and my advanced years, have been made comfortable as they have, that our connection, on the whole, has been a happy one. Loth should I be, and greatly distressed indeed, should anything take place to render it otherwise with us. I sincerely hope such will not be the effect of this communication, or of any measures to which it may naturally give rise. Unless I am greatly deceived, it is my earnest wish and prayer, that, as from the beginning the great Head of the Church has exercised over you a kind and unremitting care, so He may continue to, and that in the choice of one to serve Him in the gospel, it may be your happiness to have His discretion and influence to act judiciously, and in a manner, that shall promote your own, and the good of your children, and your children's children, and that of multitudes of others, till He shall come in power and great glory to judge the quick and the dead. All of which is respectfully submitted by your unworthy but affectionate pastor,

PAYSON WILLISTON."

This request was granted, and he was reluctantly dismissed from the active duties of the pastorate. During his ministry, he had met with a very encouraging degree of success in his noble work, and many souls had been given as seals of his ministry. But, though he no longer sustained the relation of pastor to his people, he was not idle. He loved them to the last, and was ever desirous of promoting their welfare, and many remember with pleasure the visits and kind and fatherly counsel of their aged pastor, who still loved to share with them their joys and sorrows. "His closet, the sanctuary, the meeting for social prayer, were his loved retreats, and next to these the house of his friends." For several years he was the last survivor of his class, and for some time he was the oldest graduate of Yale College. But at last his mission on earth was ended, and on the 30th of January, 1856, he was called by the Great Head of the Church to come up higher. Though spared to the age of ninety-two years and seven months, yet he, too, must die, and "as a shock of corn fully ripe" he was gathered to his rest, while many friends missed him, and greatly lamented his loss.

His funeral sermon was preached by Rev. John Woodbridge, D. D., from Prov. 13, 22: "A good man leaveth an inheritance to his children's children." He has passed away, but "he being dead yet speaketh," and the influence of his life and teachings will remain yet many years, and future generations shall hear, and honor, the name of Rev. PAYSON WILLISTON.

The next pastor of the church was Rev. Wm. Bement, a native of Ashfield, and a graduate of Dartmouth College. He was ordained on the 16th of October, 1833, by the same council that dismissed Mr. Williston. This ordination was one of the last examples of an ordination conducted after the manner of the fathers. The council assembled on the previous day, and held a prolonged public examination of the candidate, connecting devotional exercises therewith. A music teacher was on hand to prepare the choir for a great occasion. An hour before the ordination services, strings of carriages might be seen coming in from neighboring towns. The council, having assembled at an appointed place, marched in solemn procession to the meeting-house, where the waiting crowd, extending quite a distance from the front door, parted to the right and left and stood with uncovered heads until the reverend procession had passed through the broad aisle. After the conclusion of the public services, the council returned in like manner, to partake together of the dinner provided for them, and the houses of the whole parish were open for the entertainment of strangers.

On this occasion, the sermon was preached by Rev. Samuel Osgood, D. D.; the Charge to the Pastor was given by Rev. Payson Williston, D. D.; the Right Hand of Fellowship by Rev. Sumner G. Clapp; the Address to the People by Rev. Joseph Penny; and the Closing Prayer by Rev. H. P. Chapin.

The pastorate of Mr. Bement extended over a period of nearly seventeen years, and was productive of great good to the church and people. He was a faithful pastor and preacher, never shunning to declare unto his flock the whole counsel of God. The fruits of his labors still remain. He was strongly attached to his people, a public parting from whom he could not endure. He therefore wrote a most affectionate farewell address, which was read from the pulpit, about a month after his dismissal. Many will remember the occasion, and the deep and tender solicitude for them, which breathed from every sentence of the address. He left the people with the unanimous assurance, on their part, "that his departure was neither anticipated or desired by them, that they esteem him highly in love, hold his services in most grateful remembrance, and cordially approve of the views which he entertained of the Christian ministry, and of the efforts which he has made to extend the kingdom of the Redeemer."

During his ministry, an organization was formed, which took the name of the Young Men's Home Missionary

Society, which pledged itself to the support of Rev. Melzar Montague, a native of Westhampton, as a missionary in Wisconsin. Mr. Montague was ordained here, October 29, 1844, on which occasion a sermon was preached by Rev. Edward W. Hooker, D. D.

The third pastor in succession was Rev. Rollin S. Stone, a graduate of Yale College. He was installed as pastor of the church, Oct. 8, 1850, and dismissed at his own request, July 26, 1852. The sermon at his installation was preached by Rev. E. Y. Swift, now settled in Williamsburg. After his dismission, a call was extended to Rev. A. M. Colton to become pastor of the church, which he accepted, and was installed March 2, 1853, Rev. John Woodbridge, D. D., delivering a discourse from I Cor. 1, 23-4. Mr. Colton is a native of Georgia, Vt., a graduate of Yale College, and was formerly pastor of the Congregational Church in Amherst. He still labors with the people, by whom he is greatly respected and beloved. Two or three seasons of unusual religious interest have blessed the church during his pastorate, and many have been added to its numbers.

The following list shows the persons who have been deacons of the church since its organization, together with the time of their appointment, and the length of time which they held the office:—

Stephen Wright,	chosen	1786,	served	21	years.
Benjamin Lyman,	"	1786,	"	12	"
Obadiah Janes,	"	1788,	"	19	"
Joel Parsons,	"	1798,	"	15	"
Solomon Lyman,	"	1807,	"	18	"
Thaddeus Clapp,	"	1808,	"	33	"
Sylvester Lyman,	"	1813,	"	20	"
Julius Hannum,	"	1825,	"	7	"
Ithamar Clark,	"	1832,	"	25	"

Eleazer W. Hannum, chosen 1833,
Samuel Williston, " 1841, served 11 years.
Luther Wright, " 1857,
E. Alonzo Clark, " 1857.

The present church edifice was built in 1836 and '7. from a plan drawn by William F. Pratt of Northampton. Mr. Pratt and Jason Clark were the contractors. The corner stone was laid June 9, 1836. The house was dedicated March 16, 1837, on which occasion a sermon was preached from Acts 8, 49, by the pastor, Rev. Mr. Bement, Its dimensions are 80 by 50 feet, and it originally cost less than $6,000. In the autumn of 1844, owing partially to the increase of numbers, consequent upon the establishment of Williston Seminary, the church edifice was enlarged by the substitution of more capacious galleries. The building was also set back fifty feet, and at Mr. Williston's expense the spire remodeled, and built seventeen feet higher, and an organ and clock introduced. In 1865, it was removed from its original site to a location near by, and which, in some respects, was more desirable. At that time the whole interior was remodeled, the galleries lowered, the pews rebuilt, the walls neatly frescoed, a modern style of pulpit and furniture introduced, and an addition made in the rear of the house for the accommodation of the organ and choir. The repairs were made at a cost of more than $5,000.

The present number of church members is 253. The number in 1833, at the settlement of Mr. Bement, was 222.

In the year 1818, efforts were first made to establish a Sabbath School here. The project was opposed by some, on the ground that the children, if left to themselves, as they necessarily would be after the dismission of the school, would not conduct in a manner becoming the sanctity of the day; and it also was thought to be an innovation to have a school on the Sabbath; but so earnest were the friends of the enterprise that opposition finally ceased, and a school organized in the district school house that stood at the junction of Park and Main streets.

Hon. Samuel Williston and Rev. Solomon Lyman, then in early life, were largely instrumental in its establishment here, and neither they nor any others who have bestowed their efforts in the behalf of this work have seen any reason to regret the exertions which they have made. The enterprise gained in favor with the people, and has ever since been sustained. It has met with an encouraging degree of success during the thirty-eight years of its existence. A hearty co-operation on the part of the parents, not only by their sympathy, but by their presence, has been long felt by those engaged in the school to be an essential requisite to the fullest degree of success.

The communion service which is in use by the church was the gift of Mrs. Tirzah, widow of Luther Clapp. She died August 13, 1811. In her will she bequeathed $300 to the church and town, $35 of which, according to her direction, was expended in the purchase of a pall cloth, and the balance fell to the church. In 1846, a commodious brick parsonage was erected on one of the pleasantest sites in the town at an expense of $3,000, the greater portion of which was built by Mr. Williston, though the society relinquished to him the old parsonage.

The church has been blessed with many revival seasons when the renewing and sanctifying influence of the Holy Spirit have descended abundantly, bringing blessings unspeakably great and precious to the church. Particularly worthy of note are those which occurred in the years 1789, 1806, '16, '23, '28, '31, '54, '58.

THE PAYSON CHURCH AND SOCIETY.

The large increase of the population of the town, consequent upon the establishment of Williston Seminary, and the removal of the button works from Haydenville to Easthampton, was thought to render it necessary that another house of worship should be erected. The first meeting for the organization of a second church was held July 8, 1852. It was voted that the church should bear the name of the Payson Church. July 12, 1852, an invitation was extended to Rev. R. S. Stone to become the pastor of the new church and society, which was accepted. The church, consisting originally of 100 members, was organized Dec. 28th of the same year, and the church edifice dedicated in the evening of the same day. The dedication sermon was delivered by Dr. N. Adams of Boston. The services of installation were conducted as follows:—Sermon by Rev. Dr. Hitchcock of Amherst College, from Romans 9, 1—13. Charge to the pastor by Rev. Mr. Root of Williamsburg, Right Hand of Fellowship by Rev. Dr. Hall of Northampton, Installing Prayer by Rev. Mr. Judd of Whately. Address to the people by Rev. Mr. Clapp of Brattleboro, Hon. Samuel Williston and Dr. Atherton Clark were chosen deacons. E. A. Hubbard served as church clerk until 1855, when C. B. Johnson, Esq., was chosen, and he has since held that office. Seth Warner was the first treasurer of the society, and has been the treasurer of the church from its formation. Lucius Preston has for a number of years filled the office of treasurer of the society.

The church at its commencement was very unfortunate in their house of worship. Three houses have been erected, of which two were destroyed by fire, and the third partially destroyed by the falling of the steeple. The first house, which was erected in 1852, was burned on Sabbath morning, January 29, 1854, the fire having caught from the furnace. There was no insurance. The erection of the second building was commenced early the following spring, and September 1, 1854, when more than half finished, was again destroyed by fire. The walls and foundation were partially saved, but there was no insurance, and the loss was almost wholly borne by Mr. Williston. Instead of being disheartened by these losses, the society, with an energy worthy of much praise, immediately commenced the erection of a third building, which was completed in 1855, and dedicated September 6th, of that year, on which occasion a sermon was preached by Rev. Mr. Stone, from Psalms 132, 8. The cost of this house, exclusive of bell, &c., was about $14,000, which was borne by Mr. Williston. In this, as in the first case, the bell, $560, was given by Mr. Seth Warner, the organ, $2,500, by Hon. H. G. Knight, and the furniture by the society. The house was of brick, 87 by 50 feet, with a tower projection of 15 feet, and a pulpit recess of 9 feet. The spire was 163 feet in height, and of beautiful proportions. While its work of rebuilding was in progress the society held its meetings at the Town Hall. "The First church and society kindly invited their sister society to meet with them, but preferring to keep their pastor employed and their organization in good condition, and for the further reason that the house with both societies would be too crowded, the invitation was, with many thanks, declined." When the second house was destroyed, the parsonage near by was also burned. The pastor also sustained considerable loss by the destruction and damage to furniture, &c. While the third church edifice was being built, the society erected another parsonage of brick. It cost, besides the land and foundation, about $4,000. Mr. Williston and Mr. Knight each contributed $1,400 for this object.

Early in the morning of January 2, 1862, the tall spire of the church was blown down by a high wind. It fell upon the roof of the building, entirely demolishing it, and laying the interior in ruins. The organ and desk, however, escaped injury. The vestry remained unharmed, and in this room the congregation held their public services while the upper part was being rebuilt. At this time an addition was made to the building in the rear, to furnish a recess for the organ and choir behind the pulpit. "The dimensions of the present church edifice are as follows:—External length of the main body, 89 feet by 50 in width; height of spire, 163 feet; organ recess, 27 by 19 feet. The audience room is 75 by 48, below, and in the gallery 87 by 48, adding the space above the porch. The total expense of building and rebuilding the church thus far cannot fall below $50,000. By far the larger part of this has been the immediate gift of one man, the son of a poor minister, the first pastor of the First church in this place."

Rev. Mr. Stone retained his connection as pastor of the church until January 21, 1863. During his ministry over the church, extending through a period of a little more than ten years, Mr. Stone labored with zeal and fidelity for their upbuilding. He was with them during all their reverses and discouragements, and shared these in sympathy with his people. His ministry was blessed in the hopeful conversion of many. The addition of converts averaged about one a month during this time, though at a little more than half the communion seasons there were no additions.

In the fall of the same year, the church and society extended an invitation to Rev. S. T. Seelye, D. D., of Albany, to become their pastor. He accepted the invitation, and was installed October 14, 1863. Since that time he has continued to labor among the people, by whom he is held in high esteem. His labors have been blessed with much success, and many have been added to the church. Its present number of members is 345, of whom 113 are males, and 232 females. The additions during 1865 were 33 on profession and 10 by letter. The number dismissed was 20, died 7, making a net gain of 16 during the year.

The following persons have been chosen to fill the office of deacon since the organization of the church :—Dr. Atherton Clark, Nov. 14, 1852; Samuel Williston, Nov. 14, 1852; Charles B. Johnson, Aug. 29, 1861; Ansel B. Lyman, Aug. 29, 1861; Seth Warner, June 2, 1864; E. A. Hubbard, June 2, 1864; E. H. Sawyer, March 1, 1866.

THE METHODIST CHURCH AND SOCIETY.

The establishment of the manufacturing business here brought into the town a number of persons connected with the Methodist denomination. The growth of the town, it was thought, would soon necessitate the erection of another house of worship. Rev. Mr. Potter, a preacher connected with the Methodist Conference, was engaged, and meetings were held on the Sabbath in the Town Hall. This was in the year 1850 or '51. The enterprise, however, did not meet with sufficient success to warrant the formation of a society, and after a time it was abandoned. Many of its friends became connected with the Payson church on its organization soon after. For ten years nothing more was done by this denomination. During the fall and winter of 1862, prayer meetings were established in private houses by a few individuals, which awakened considerable religious interest. This interest extended, and meetings were held in a hall provided for that purpose. During the progress of this work of grace, large numbers were awakened, and very many professed an interest in Christ.

The preliminary steps in the formation of a society were taken in the last of '62. Its organization was fully effected in April, 1863, when Rev. S. Jackson was appointed its first pastor. This new movement soon commended itself to public confidence, by the good it was accomplishing, particularly among those not hitherto reached by the other societies.

At a town meeting held in the fall of 1864, the town, with great liberality, donated to the society a piece of land in the center of the village, on which to erect a house of worship.

Late in the summer of 1865 they broke ground for the erection of a church, 50 by 80 feet, and the work of building has been pushed forward with commendable rapidity, till the exterior is at present nearly completed. The style is somewhat unique in this section of the state, being the "pure early English Gothic," the style immediately following the "Norman Gothic," and preceding the "decorated English Gothic," and "a favorite on account of its purity and simplicity." The estimated cost is $13,000. It is expected to be completed early in the ensuing fall. The society numbers about 350. The church membership is nearly 150.

In the spring of 1866, Rev. Mr. Jackson was called to labor elsewhere, and the church is now under the pastoral care of Rev. Franklin Furber. Mr. Jackson was highly esteemed during his stay here, not only among his own people, but throughout the community.

CHAPTER III.

EDUCATIONAL INTERESTS.

PUBLIC SCHOOLS.

The first school which was taught in town, of which we have any reliable record, was at Pascommuck, in the year 1739. At that time, Northampton appropriated a sum of money for a school there. There is no account of any further appropriation until 1748. In this year, and in nearly every subsequent year, they gave money for schooling at Bartlett's Mill, and at Pascommuck. The wages of teachers in those times appear small in comparison with what teachers now receive. Six shillings a week were paid to Obadiah Janes, Philip Clark, Joel Parsons and others for keeping school in their own districts, when they boarded themselves. If the teacher lived out of the district more was sometimes paid. Then only the rudiments of education, as they are now considered, were taught. Perhaps, however, their education was as sufficient for the wants of those times as is ours for the wants of the present day. Science and literary culture were comparatively little advanced, while popular education was, as it were, still in its infancy. At all events, this training prepared them to perform well their part in cherishing the liberties which the Pilgrim Fathers sought in coming to these shores.

At a meeting of the freeholders of Easthampton soon

after its incorporation, £15 were raised for the use of schools, of which, at this time, there were probably but three. The same sum was annually appropriated until 1793, when it was increased to £20. Since that time the pecuniary provision for schools has more than kept pace with the increasing number of children.

In 1807	$200	were raised for the use of schools.
" 1820	220	" " "
" 1830	300	" " "
" 1840	360	" " "
" 1850	600	" " "
" 1860	1200	" " "
" 1865	2200	" " "
" 1866	3500	" " "

Besides the sum raised in 1866 for the support of schools, the sum of $3800 was appropriated for building new school houses.

In 1797 the town was first divided into school districts, of which there were four. Nashawannuck comprised that section of the town bounded on the south by Manhan river, and west by Saw-mill brook. The West district was bounded on the south by Manhan river, and east by Saw-mill brook. Pascommuck was bounded on the north by Manhan river, and on the west by Broad brook. The Center district comprised nearly all the remaining portion, though a few families in the extreme southeastern part were included in no district. At a later period the town was divided into six districts.

At first the management of the school was left entirely in the hands of the district, the money raised by the town being equitably apportioned to the several districts, and by them spent according to their discretion. Later, however, a general committee was appointed, whose duty it was to examine teachers, and visit the schools to inquire into their progress. The hiring of teachers, the disbursement of the money, and the ownership of the school houses were still in the hands of the district. In 1864, by vote of the town, the districts were abolished, and the whole control of the schools passed into the hands of the general committee, the town purchasing the school houses of the several districts. To this measure there was considerable opposition, and time will be required to show whether or not it was a wise course.

In the spring of 1864, it was voted to establish a high school, and a sum of money appropriated to purchase a site, and provide materials for the erection of a suitable building for this purpose. The building was completed in the summer of 1865, at a total cost of $15,000. It was dedicated August 29, 1865. The building is a very fine one, and an ornament to the place. It is capable of accommodating 212 scholars.

The rapid increase in the population of the town has called for the erection of several new school houses. During the past year, there were 12 schools held, with an aggregate attendance during the summer and fall terms of 518.

WILLISTON SEMINARY.

Any notice of the leading features in the history of Easthampton would not be complete without mention of the Seminary established there by the extraordinary munificence of the Hon. Samuel Williston.

"This Institution," says Mr. Luther Wright, in his Historical Sketch of Easthampton, "originated in a desire to extend the advantages of a thorough training in the elements of an English and classical education. The idea of such a school was suggested sometime before the close of 1840; but it was not fully and finally decided to found and locate it here till December of that year, or in January, 1841. In February following, it was incorporated with the power to hold $50,000 for educational purposes. It was opened for the admission of students Dec. 2, 1841.

"The founder of this Seminary and its early friends, hoped that the existence of such a school, of the high order they contemplated, would greatly promote the interests of Academical education in Western Massachusetts. It was not their aim merely to multiply Academies. These, such as they were, were already quite numerous enough in this region. But they had either a very small endowment, or none at all; and were generally farmed or let out to teachers, who kept up schools, in the best way they could, through the year, or a part of it. There could seldom be any division of labor in teaching, for want of funds to procure a suitable number of competent teachers. The minds of the teachers were often distracted by the many recitations they were obliged to hear, in a manner as unsatisfactory to themselves as to their pupils. And then, again, there was a lack of discipline in these Academies generally, so essential to the existence of a good school. It was not strange that the motive to have as large a number as possible connected with the Academy—because the more students the more salary—should often have had too strong an influence in retaining scholars. And as no school can be distinguished for thoroughness of instruction unless equally marked in its character for strictness of discipline, it was deemed an object of great moment to the interests of education in this region that an academical institution should be established, with a sufficient endowment, on the one hand, to allow the employment of an adequate number of competent teachers, with the necessary divison of labor in teaching; and on the other hand, that these teachers should be independent in the control and government of their pupils. Strictness in discipline, and thoroughness in instruction, with the word of God, were to constitute the true basis of the new institution. Its crowning excellence was to consist of a faithful application, on the part of the teachers, of the great principles of the Bible to the consciences, intellects and hearts of their pupils. Unless the above named objects were kept steadily in view by the teachers, and as steadily pursued, the existence of the Seminary was not demanded. With these sure elements of prosperity, and amply endowed, as it may be, to enable the teachers to accomplish the designs in view, its establishment was regarded, at the time it was founded, as an object of the highest importance. The fact, that, within a few years after it went into operation, thousands of our youth had availed themselves of its advantages, is evidence of the high estimation in which it was held by the public, and also of the wisdom of its establishment. Of these thousands, many have completed their collegiate course, many others are now in college, while several hundred more, having been greatly aided here in qualifying themselves as teachers in our common schools, have been and still are engaged in that important sphere of duty. One great object in view in the establishment of the Seminary, was to raise up and qualify common school teachers for their employment."

In the Constitution of the Seminary, Mr. Williston, in the exercise of a just regard for the moral as well as the intellectual welfare of the members of the school, throws about them these wholesome restrictions:—

"And in particular, no student shall board in any profane or otherwise vicious family, or where intoxicating drinks are sold or used as a beverage, or where the influence of the family is, in any way, prejudicial to the morals of youth, or hostile to the great interests of the Seminary.

"To preclude all misunderstanding of the design of Williston Seminary, I declare again in conclusion, that the primary and principal object of the Institution is the glory of God in the extension of the Christian Religion, and in the promotion of true piety among men; that the discipline of the mind in all its noble faculties is, and should be deemed, next in importance; and that in subservience to these paramount ends, the several branches of useful knowledge, above mentioned, should be assiduously cultivated. Accordingly, I hereby ordain and require that the school exercises of each day shall be opened and closed with the reading of the Scriptures and prayer; that at some convenient and suitable hour of each week an exercise in the Bible, either a lecture or recitation, as may be thought best, shall be held for the benefit of the whole school; that, by precept and example, the teachers shall encourage the pupils in holding occasional meetings for social religious worship; and at other times and in other ways they shall take frequent opportunities to impart moral and religious instruction to the members of the Seminary. And that all these efforts may not be thwarted by the influence of bad members, it is proper and indispensable that great pains be taken, both by trustees and teachers, for the prompt removal, by private dismission or public expulsion, as the case may require, of any incorrigibly indolent, disorderly, profane, or otherwise vicious youth from all connection with the Seminary."

The first Principal of the Institution was Rev. Luther Wright, a native of the town, and one who sympathized fully with the founder in the object aimed at in the establishment of the school, and in the method by which that end was to be attained. Indeed, it may be said that to him in no small degree is the town and the community indebted for its establishment here, and for its success. The original building, which was of wood, was burned March 4, 1857. Its place was supplied with a large brick building, completed near the close of the same year, at a cost of about $20,000.

Before this time, however, a second building, constructed of brick, had been erected, in which the chemical and philosophical department found accommodation. In it there was also a large school-room, and a recitation room adjoining, while the upper story and wing were occupied for student's rooms.

In the fall of 1863, the foundation for a gymnasium was laid. Owing partly to a scarcity of building materials, it was not completed and ready for occupancy until the summer term of 1865. It may safely be said to be one of the finest gymnasiums in the country, and the excellent opportunity it affords to students for regular systematic exercise, cannot fail to be beneficial, and it certainly adds another attraction to the many which the institution already possessed. It has on the lower floor four bowling alleys, besides adjoining rooms for recitation, for washing, and for dressing. In the upper part is a capacious gallery for spectators, besides the floor for exercise. The structure is 80x50 feet, with a tower 102 feet in height, and cost, together with the land, over $20,000.

Last year the chemical laboratory was entirely remodeled, and new apparatus purchased, for which $2,500 was expended. In the philosophical department, also, new apparatus was obtained, to the amount of $3,000. A new dormitory, which is to be of brick, and four stories in height, is in process of erection. It stands near where the First Congregational church stood, and is to be erected at an estimated cost of $50,000. With the exception of one school-room, it is to be occupied with sleeping paartments. The buildings, grounds, apparatus, fixtures, furniture and working capital of the institution, will amount to not less than $225,000.

In 1863, Rev. Josiah Clark, who was the second Principal of the Seminary, which place he had held during a period of fourteen years, resigned his position, much to the regret of the members of the Seminary, and others. He was succeeded by Rev. Marshall Henshaw, who had been Professor of Mathematics and Natural Philosophy in Rutgers College. He still occupies the post, and since his appointment has discharged its duties with fidelity.

During the twenty-five years of the existence of the Institution, a large number of students have here laid the foundation for a classical education, many of whom are now engaged as ministers of the gospel at home or abroad, and a still larger number, probably, have here studied the advanced branches of an English course. The Seminary has many times, especially during its early history, been blessed with the gracious outpourings of God's spirit, when many have been led to the Saviour.

Its influence, through those who have gone forth from it, has been very wide spread, and, from its large endowment, we can feel assured that this influence will be permanent.

CHAPTER IV.

EARLY CIVIL AND MILITARY HISTORY.

We have now considered the early history of the town, the hardships which our fathers endured, and the perils which they encountered from the hostile Indians. We have seen their incorporation as a district, differing only from a town in that they were denied the right of representation. We have followed out the history of the original church, and of those since founded. What remains to be said of its subsequent history will perhaps be more conveniently given under different heads, which will be successively presented.

A remarkable unanimity of sentiment has always prevailed among its inhabitants, on political subjects. In the time of Jefferson, and before, the town was strongly federal. Not more than six or eight votes were cast for the candidates for the Democratic party. After the Federalist party became extinct in name, the Whigs, who held, in the main, their principles, were greatly in the ascendant; and, since the organization of the Republican party, it has polled about nine-tenths of the vote of the town.

While, however, the people have been as enthusiastic in their political associations and preferences as those of any other section, these have not exercised a controlling influence in the choice of town officers. Here, merit and fitness for office, rather than party feeling, have directed in the selection.

In the early Indian and the Revolutionary wars, the history of this town is identified with that of Northampton. The citizens of this section, however, contributed their full proportion of men and means.

Rev. Luther Wright, in his historical sketch of Easthampton, from which, by the way, together with the half century sermon of Rev. Mr. Williston, we have derived much assistance, says :—"It is not known exactly how many, from what is now Easthampton, were engaged in the war of the Revolution. It is certain that among those engaged more or less in the service of their country, were Capt. Joseph Clapp and Quartermaster Benjamin Clapp, Dr. Stephen Wood and his sons, Daniel and David; the father died in the service at West Point; John Clapp, who was in the army four years, Benjamin Lyman, Jr., Stephen Wright, Jr., David Clapp, who never returned, Levi Clapp, Eliakim Clark, afterwards Captain, Moses Gouch, Barzillai Brewer, and Willet Chapman. The last two died in the army."

SHAY'S REBELLION.

The first event which necessitated the calling forth of troops, after the Revolutionary war, was Shay's rebellion. The expenses which had been incurred in carrying on the war, the depreciation in value of paper currency, the heavy taxation, and the extent of public and private indebtedness, all contributed to bring about a state of popular discontent. The amount of individual liabilities, and the consequent legal action on the part of creditors to recover their dues, had caused the people to grow restive under their burdens.

As is usual in such times, the government was held responsible for the distress. There were also certain demagogues, who were ready to embrace any opportunity to advance their own interests, by whatever means. Prominent among these was Daniel Shay. These added fuel to the flame. Criminal courts were broken up at various places, by lawless mobs. Conventions of the people were held, to consider the grievances. Although these, at first, disclaimed all connection with these riotous proceedings, they only fanned the flame of discontent. Not content with breaking up the inferior courts, they attempted to break up the Supreme Judicial Court at Springfield ; but their designs were anticipated, and soldiers provided for the emergency. Among these was a company of about twenty, commanded by Capt. David Lyman and Lieut. Noah Janes. We have been unable to find a record of the names of the members of this company, but it is believed that the following list comprises nearly all :—Lemuel Lyman, Elijah Wright, Gideon Wright, Stephen Wright, Levi Clapp, Thaddeus Clapp, Eleazar Hannum, Justice Lyman, Eliakim Clark, Eleazar Clark, Enos Janes, Silas Brown, Arad Brown, Job Strong, Israel Phelps, Zadok Danks.

The rebellion culminated in an attempt to capture the arsenal on Springfield hill. It was on the 25th of January, 1787. The post was commanded by Gen. Shepard, with 800 government troops. He warned the insurgents, as they were advancing, to desist, but they gave no heed. He then ordered his artillery to be fired, first at their right, then at their left, and then over their heads, all of which was done without effect. A volley was then fired among them, when they dispersed. When it was known that this attack was meditated, a small company of men, raised in Southampton and Easthampton, started to reinforce the government troops, but they were captured by a detachment of the insurrectionists. They were, however, only held in custody two or three days, in consequence of the defeat at Springfield. There was but a single person in Easthampton who was active in the rebellion, and but few who sympathized with it, and these were the old tories of the Revolution.

The people felt that their liberties had been gained at too dear a price of blood and treasure, for them to surrender them into the hands of a few demagogues, or to lift their hands against the state, even though there were some causes of dissatisfaction.

THE WAR OF 1812.

When the second war with England arose, the citizens of this town, in common with other parts of New England, opposed it. They regarded the mother country as "struggling against a monster of political iniquity, whose success they regarded as the greatest of all political evils." That there were grievances, they did not doubt. But they believed that England never would have resorted to the impressment of seamen, except to save herself from the grasp of France. They considered an appeal to arms as the last resort of an aggrieved party. At a meeting of the town, July 6, 1812, it was voted to oppose a war with England. Voted, also, that the selectmen be a committee to send a memorial to Congress, and also "a committee of safety, to receive information for public safety, upon public affairs." Thaddeus Clapp was appointed a delegate to the county convention, held at Northampton, for the purpose of "considering the duty of government upon the war question." Their opposition to the war was only in principle, and did not lead them to any acts of open resistance. A company was called for from Southampton and Easthampton, to go to Boston and defend it against an anticipated attack from the British. The following persons were drafted:—John Alpress, Elisha Alvord, Worcester Avery, Levi Brown,

George Clapp, James Clapp, Philip Clark, Gershon Danks, Stephen Hendrick, Moses Gouch, Luther Pomeroy, Spencer Pomeroy, Jesse Ring, Harris Wight, Collins Wood, Ebenezer Wood. Thaddeus Parsons was Lieutenant of the Company.

Jesse Coats of this town, was at the same time a member of the Northampton Artillery Company, which did service at the same time.

CHAPTER V.

MANUFACTURES.

Agriculture being the principal employment of the people, manufactures received but little attention until the year 1847, when Mr. Williston commenced his operations at Broad Brook. There is however, one branch of that department of industry which, although less important and now out of date, deserves a passing notice.

Probably about the year 1780, Jonathan Clapp commenced the business of fulling cloth. He occupied a portion of the grist-mill, where for a number of years he carried on the business, receiving the cloth which had been woven in the various families of the surrounding towns, and "fulling" it, as it was termed, an operation by which it was thickened and rendered firmer. The customary charge for fulling was three cents a yard. After undergoing this operation, it needed to be "dressed" to render it fit for clothing.

Soon after, Capt. Joseph Clapp built a fulling mill on Broad Brook, a short distance below the button and suspender factories, where he not only fulled cloth, but colored and dressed it, for which he charged twenty-five cents per yard. There were but few mills of this description in this region, and hence he carried on quite a flourishing business.

In the year 1792, or 1793, Thaddeus Clapp, son of Joseph, went to Worthington, and engaged in this business, but in consequence of a failure of his supply of water, he soon returned and entered into copartnership with his father. This relation existed until the death of the latter in 1797, when the works were removed to Manhan river near the grist-mill. After the business was given up by Mr. Clapp it was conducted successively by Roswell Knight, by Lowell E. and Jason Janes, then by Janes & Alvord, and lastly by Janes & Ferry. In 1835, by the last named persons the old shop was torn down, and the building, now occupied by H. B. Shoals, as a tannery, was erected for the manufacture of satinet. It was filled with machinery and run until 1837, when cloths were sold for less than the first cost of the wool. The works were consequently suspended. The first power loom ever run in this town was started in that mill. When hand looms were superseded by water power looms, the necessity for mills of this description ceased to exist. They had performed their part in the progress of manufactures, and must give way before its further advance. Its priority of date, and not its extent, entitles this branch to the first mention, for when it is compared with the extensive manufacturing interests of the town at present, it seems small indeed.

The real history of this branch of industry in this town, may be said to have commenced with Hon. Samuel Williston, who is known abroad, not so much as a man of business and wealth, as he is as a munificent patron of education. Williston Seminary, which he founded, and which ranks second to none in the land as a preparatory school, —Amherst College, which holds no unenviable position among the first class colleges in the country, a position which it owes in no small degree to his benefactions,—Mt.

Holyoke Seminary, pioneer and princess among institutions for the advanced education of young women,—these have given him his reputation, and tell the story better than words of ours can do. But the ability to do all this he owes, under God, to his great success as a manufacturer.

He commenced the sewed button business here, as early as 1827, and continued it for quite a number of years. With good management it constantly increased. At one time he gave employment to as many as a thousand families, who resided in towns as far north as Hatfield, east to Granby, south to West Springfield, and west to Peru. He also engaged somewhat largely in the manufacture of silk twist buttons. They were made by winding twist upon wooden molds of different shapes and sizes. They were used upon expensive garments, and hence did not take the place of sewed buttons. In 1836, while in New York making sales, he came across some buttons imported from England, called the "Florentine flexible shank button." The thought suggested itself to his mind, that they might as well be made here as in England, and, with this idea, he purchased a quantity of them, brought them home, and carried them to Messrs. Joel and Josiah Hayden of Williamsburg, who had made a large quantity of button molds for him. An engagement was entered into, according to which they were to invent the machinery, and manufacture the buttons, while he was to furnish the money and make the sales; they were to undertake the mechanical, and he the commercial part, and the profits were to be shared.

This business was comparatively new in this country. Several attempts had been made to manufacture buttons covered by machinery, but the degree of success which had rewarded these endeavors was not such as to encourage the further continuance of the enterprise, which required the most complicated machinery and the most skillful management. The work was however undertaken, and the winter of 1833–4 was spent in efforts to invent and construct the proper machinery.

In the early part of 1834, Mr. Williston met, in New York, Francis Sidney, a Creole, who had been employed in one of the large button manufacturing establishments in England, and understood the making of buttons. He was engaged to come to Haydenville and assist in constructing the machinery, in which work he rendered essential aid. He introduced a radical change in the character of the button machinery, as it had been before employed and attempted, and was the author of some of the distinctive features of the business as since carried on, though no process of his introduction is now in use.

By the 4th of July one covering machine was in readiness, and on that day the first buttons were covered by Miss Elvira Clapp of Southampton. This was the beginning of the button business as it now exists here. It speaks highly for the mechanical skill and ingenuity of the Messrs. Hayden, and of those machinists whom they employed, that they were able to ensure success to an enterprise so fraught with difficulty, as the invention and construction of machinery for making buttons.

In a few years, Josiah Hayden sold out his interest in the concern to his brother, and in 1847 Mr. Williston bought the interest of Joel Hayden, and in the following year transferred the works to Easthampton, where he erected a building 97 by 45 feet, three stories high, besides an attic. About this time he took in Horatio G. Knight and afterwards Seth Warner as partners. Since that time, the business has been carried on by the firm of Williston, Knight & Co., until Dec. 1, 1865, when the

5*

partnership expired, and a stock company, called the "National Button Company," was formed, with a capital of $150,000. Of this company Mr. Williston is President, and its Treasurer is Mr. Knight, who for a number of years has been the active manager of the business.

The manufacture of sewed buttons did not entirely cease with the introduction of the "flexible shank button," but they were gradually superseded by them, so that the former are now entirely out of date.

This company gives employment to 125 hands, and turns out 1200 gross of buttons daily, of over 300 kinds, including shape, size, quality, color and material. They expect soon to be able to produce 1500 gross daily. A great deal of silk and brocade fabric is used, which renders the material quite costly. The value of stock annually consumed is $60,000, and that of the manufactured products $160,000. The building at present occupied is 106 by 30 feet, with a wing 40 by 20. It was built in 1861. At that time the one at first erected was leased to the Goodyear Elastic Fabric Co.

The button business requires close calculation, and rigid economy in its management. There has been from the first great competition, both in the sewed and manufactured button. It is a fact worthy of note, that almost all who have embarked in the enterprise have failed.

In 1848 and 9, Mr. Williston erected a brick building by the side of the button factory, to be occupied in the manufacture of suspender webbing, which business he continued in his own name until 1852, when he sold out to a joint stock company, which had obtained a charter from the Legislature.

It assumed the name of the Nashawannuck Manufacturing Co. Mr. Williston has been President, and E. H. Sawyer, Treasurer and Agent, since its first organization. These gentlemen, together with H. G. Knight, are the principal stockholders who reside in Easthampton, while there are large owners of stock in New York, Boston, and other places.

The capital of the company was originally $100,000, was afterwards at different periods increased to $125,000, $140,000, and $200,000, and is now $300,000 while they have been empowered by the Legislature to increase the capital to $500,000.

At the time of their organization the company purchased the right to use Chas. Goodyear's vulcanized rubber in all kinds of woven goods. This purchase almost gave them the monopoly of this branch of business, and has contributed largely to their success. They afterward disposed of this right to the Goodyear Elastic Fabric Co., and the Glendale Vulcanized Rubber Co., reserving to themselves only the right to use it in suspenders and frills.

The business flourished in their hands to such an extent, that in 1855 it became necessary to erect another building to supply their increasing trade. In 1856 they purchased of Atwater & Bristol their suspender works in New Haven, and for four years manufactured goods in that place. In 1860 that property was destroyed by fire, at considerable loss. Instead of rebuilding there they put up a factory here, filling the space between the two others occupied by them, thus making one continuous structure 315 feet in length, and about 40 in breadth, to which is now added a wing extending back. In addition to this, they occupy a large three story building as an office, finishing and store room, together with several smaller buildings in the rear of the main factory. Until 1860 they used the lower floor of Williston, Knight, & Co.'s button factory, in the manufacture of cotton yarn for their own use. Such was their increase of business, however, that they were obliged to purchase monthly several thousand dollars worth of cotton yarn, and it was therefore thought best to abandon the making of yarn altogether. Accordingly they disposed of their cotton spinning machinery to Mr. Williston, who was then contemplating the establishment of this branch of business here.

A little later they organized a new company for the manufacture of rubber thread, to which they sold their rubber machinery, and entirely relinquished this department of their manufactures, thus confining themselves more closely to their own proper work, the weaving of suspenders and other webbing.

This company whose beginnings were small, has prospered exceedingly. Its stock has been very valuable and its dividends large. In the aggregate they have turned out an immense amount of goods of the best quality. The increase of business may be seen in the fact, that, in 1852, they manufactured and sold goods to the amount of only $100,000, while in 1865 the value of manufactured products was about $1,200,000, which, even considering the enhanced prices of these times, is a large increase.

They are now owners of all the real estate which they occupy, having recently bought of Mr. Williston that portion of it which they previously rented; and they now own about half the water power at the upper mills, which is sufficient for all their purposes. The present capacity of their works is 4000 dozen pair of suspenders per week, and, in addition to this, about 50,000 yards of frills and other narrow webbing.

They own thirty-two tenements and four boarding houses, run about 150 looms, and, during the year 1865, paid for yarn, $238,000; for buckles, $35,000; about $15,000 for dye-stuffs; and $72,000 for rubber thread, while for labor, their expenditure amounted to $83,000 together with nearly $40,000 paid by the finishing department for the making up of suspenders from the webbing. Their revenue tax during the same year was $42,209. The number of hands to whom regular employment is given is 300 in addition to which about one thousand families are engaged, more or less in stitching suspenders.

In the spring of 1859, Mr. Williston commenced the erection of a building for the manufacture of cotton yarn, partly for the supply of the Nashawannuck Co. The location was about three fourths of a mile from the other factories in a northerly direction, on the same stream, where for many years a saw mill had stood.

The ground was very rough and uneven, and a large amount of grading was required to be done before the foundation could be laid. When this had been partially done, and work upon the foundation was progressing, an unexpected obstacle presented itself in the shape of a boiling spring. This threw out large quantities of water, and for a time seemed to defy all efforts to lay a solid foundation, and to build a dam. At last this difficulty seemed to have been overcome, and work on the building went forward. In about a year from its beginning it was finished, and work commenced.

But this spring, and the surrounding bed of quicksand, were destined to give still further trouble. In consequence of these, the water in the pond undermined the dam, and carried it off, together with a part of the factory. This took place shortly after its completion. Thus, not only was a heavy loss incurred, but work in the mill was delayed several months. Mr. Williston, however, set resolutely about repairing the breach, which he completed by winter. This time, no attempt was made to build a dam in the old place, but it was constructed a short distance further up the stream, and the water brought to the mill in a canal. It seemed now that this arrangement might be permanent; but here again they were doomed to disappointment. In March, 1863, the water burst through the bank of the canal, near the trunk which conveyed the water to the water wheel. It tore away the road, and did considerable damage. One engine was already in the mill, and another was immediately obtained, so that operations in the mill were only suspended for a few days. Repairs on the dam, which was at this time rebuilt in its original place, occupied four or five months.

Before this event, the cost of the establishment, including tenements, water privileges, &c., was upwards of $100,000. Since that time, the capacity of the mill has been more than doubled by large additions. It has eleven thousand spindles, and gives employment to more than 175 hands. The quantity of cotton consumed annually is about 550,000 pounds, and the capital invested, $250,000. The yarn spun is of the finest quality, equal to the best English. It is twisted under water. The mill, taken as a whole, is one of the best of its kind in America, probably the only one in the state. The machinery is of the most approved patents. Quite a village has sprung up about the mill, where, a few years ago, were no houses. About fifty tenements are owned by the company, which consists of S. Williston, J. Sutherland, and M. H. Leonard.

Their increasing business demanded the erection of a new factory, preparations for which were begun in the summer of 1865. On the 15th of August, the first stone of the foundation was laid, and in four months the walls were up, and the building covered. It is 200 by 68 feet, and is four stories high, besides an attic. It is the largest building in town, and its capacity is 18,000 spindles, and will give employment to about 200 hands. The estimated production of the new mill, when in full operation, is about the same in quantity as in the other, though the yarn and thread made is to be finer than in that. The working capital of the company, including the factories, tenements, machinery, land, &c., when the whole establishment is complete, will be between $700,000 and and $800,000.

In 1861, the Goodyear Elastic Fabric Co. was formed, whose principal business was the manufacture of elastic cloth, to be used in shoes. They leased the mill, originally occupied by Williston, Knight & Co., and carried on their operations there until recently, when they sold out to the Glendale Manufacturing Company.

In 1862, a company, consisting of H. G. Knight and E. H. Sawyer, of Easthampton, and Wm. and C. G. Judson, of New York, was organized under the title of the Glendale Vulcanized Rubber Co., with a capital of $50,000. Their business was the manufacture of elastic cord, frills, &c., which they commenced at Glendale, on the Manhan river, in the western portion of the town. They enlarged and occupied a building which had been erected by Gregory & Wells, for the manufacture of twine and batting.

In 1864, a large brick factory was erected near the railroad depot in Easthampton, by the Rubber Thread Co., the two upper stories of which the Glendale Co. rented, and now occupy. In April, 1865, the capital of this company was increased to $100,000, and in June of the same year, to $250,000, at which time they bought out the Goodyear Elastic Fabric Co. They now employ about 350 hands, and consume stock at the rate of about $250,000 per annum. They manufacture elastic cloth for shoes, all kinds of elastic cord, frills, &c. They now occupy four mills with the exception of the lower story of one of them. Their business is rapidly increasing, and quite likely will soon call for a further increase of capital. The President of this company is C. G. Judson, of New York, and its Treasurer, J. S. Lovering, of Boston. Both the Glendale and the Nashawannuck companies now obtain their rubber from the Easthampton Rubber-Thread Co., which was formed in the fall of 1863, with H. G. Knight as its President, and Seth Warner Treasurer and general Agent. Its capital is $100,000. They carry on work in the lower story of the factory erected by them, employ about twenty hands, and supply nearly all the manufacturers in the country, who employ rubber thread in their business. The amount of rubber consumed during the last six months has been about 100,000 pounds.

Mention should be made of the Gas Co., which was organized September 7, 1864, with a capital of $20,000. On the 23d of April, 1866, it was increased to $30,000. E. Ferry is President of the company, and Horace L. Clark, Treasurer.

Thus, in less than twenty years from the erection of the first factory by Mr. Williston, a manufacturing interest has grown up here, which employs, or will probably soon employ, $1,600,000 capital, and which paid during the year 1865, not less than $100,000 revenue tax. By the census of May, 1865, it appears that the manufacturing concerns in the town, employed $850,000 capital, consumed stock annually to the value of $1,247,000, and produced goods to the value of $1,675,000. The increase of capital since that time, will be attended by an increase of consumption and production, though, perhaps, not in a full ratio of that increase. These amounts appear somewhat larger than they otherwise would, from the fact that a portion of what is given as manufactured product by two of the companies, appears as stock consumed by two others.

The figures are, of course, further enhanced by the present high prices; but the quantity of stock consumed, and of goods produced, will, no doubt, go on increasing with the material growth of our country.

As intimately connected with the manufacturing interest we may with propriety notice here the First National Bank of Easthampton, which was organized April 29, 1864, with a capital of $150,000. Mr. Williston has held the office of President, and Mr. Knight that of Vice President since its organization. E. A. Hubbard was the first Cashier, a position which he resigned on his appointment as superintendent of the public schools in Springfield. Chas. E. Williams is at present its Cashier.

There is another enterprise, which, though not strictly connected with manufactures, may yet be mentioned here as properly as anywhere.

Upon the south end of Mount Tom there are two springs, which discharge daily between six and ten thousand gallons of exceedingly pure cold water. It is proposed to bring this water into the village, both for the use of families and travellers, and to furnish protection against fires. The springs have been purchased, and preliminary surveys have been made by which it has been found that they are at an elevation of about seventy feet above the plain on which the churches and other public buildings stand. This elevation would carry the water about to the height of the face of the clock on the Payson Church, and furnish abundant head for the distribution of the water all over the village to any required height. The matter is in the hands of energetic men, and this desirable work will no doubt be soon accomplished.

CHAPTER VI.

OTHER INDUSTRIAL INTERESTS.

AGRICULTURE.

Agriculture has, until recently, been the employment of a large majority of the inhabitants of the town, and an occupation so conducive to health and morality has not been without its good effect on the character of the people. Nature has not perhaps favored us more highly than other portions of our own New England; her gifts have not fallen here in greater profusion than in some other parts of our state; our soil has none of the bountiful fertility of the western prairies, or the sunny south; but the native energy of the New England character, combined with improved methods of culture, have in some measure compensated for this deficiency. Though the farming population here, as elsewhere, cannot boast of such rapid accumulation of wealth, as many engaged in other occupations, yet, when once acquired, it is not so uncertain as theirs, nor so much affected by those changes in government and trade, which occasion fluctuations in the mercantile and commercial world. The improvement in farming implements has been steady and constant. Where in the days of our early fathers, we saw the huge, unwieldy, inefficient wooden plough, requiring an expenditure of considerable force to draw it, when not impeded by the soil, now we see the most improved patterns of light, easy draught, and skillfully adapted for lightening the soil. Mowing machines are coming almost universally into use. The sickle has long ago been superseded by the cradle, and that in turn may give place to the reaper. Through the agency of machines, horse-power is being substituted for that of the hand. The old wasting systems of culture are giving way to more economical ones, and products which were once considered useless, are now turned to valuable account.

While our fathers appear thus at a disadvantage by comparison, we must bear in mind, that in the main, it was their misfortune and not their fault. Manufactures had scarcely sprung into existence, and necessity compelled them sometimes to provide implements for themselves as best they could. They did not at first fully realize the importance of enriching the soil; their principal care had been to clear up lands and prepare them for tillage. Gradually, however, they began to see that those elements must be returned to the soil which the plants abstracted from it. Soils which had hitherto produced good crops of wheat, were now found to be capable of yielding only rye, and lands on which the grass had grown spontaneously, became less productive, and needed re-seeding. Two products, wheat and flax, which have been cultivated quite extensively, have almost ceased to be raised. The lands seem better suited for other grains than for wheat, while the cultivation of flax has gone entirely into disuse. With the former cheap prices of cotton, and the immense facilities for the manufacture of cloth, flax, and the hand-looms of fifty years ago, were ruled out of existence.

Potatoes were not formerly cultivated to any extent. In 1744, Benjamin Lyman raised six bushels of potatoes, and it was a topic of remark all over Northampton. People wondered what he could do with so many potatoes.

Fruit has not received that attention which its importance demands, yet we are happy to record the fact, that lately there has been an improvement in this respect. Within a few years a large number of apple-trees have been planted, while the pear and the grape are receiving more attention.

In February, 1858, the Easthampton Farmers' Club was organized to promote the interests of the farming community, by the holding of meetings, and interchange of views and experiences. The meetings of the society have since been attended by many, with much interest and profit. Several exhibitions of fruit, vegetables, and stock have been held, which were very successful, and reflected great credit upon the members. We hope that in the future, as in the past, the association may be the means of stimulating its members to carry the department of agriculture to a still higher degree of perfection.

Rev. Luther Wright, C. B. Johnson, Esq., Ahira Lyman, and Quartus P. Lyman, have successively held the office of President of the Club, and Ansel B. Lyman, Henry Lyman, Daniel W. Lyman, and James H. Lyman, that of Secretary.

The following statistics, taken from the census of 1865, will be interesting :—

The number of farms of five acres and upwards is 135, containing 5,828 acres, of which 3,524 are improved. The total value of the farms, including buildings, is $385,550. The total value of the agricultural products is $123,000. The number of persons employed in farming, 177. The principal farm products are corn, of which there were raised 7,447 bushels ; rye, 3,255 ; oats, 2,217 ; potatoes, 9,889 ; tobacco, 136,946 pounds ; hay, 1,162 tons. Value of horses, $25,899 ; cattle, $8,080 ; cows, $13,060. Butter and milk, $5,608. Pounds of dressed meat, 149,-

028. The value of the tobacco crop, we are sorry to say, exceeds that of any other. We sincerely hope the day may not be distant when our most fertile lands may be devoted to the production of some crop useful rather than deleterious to man.

THE MERCANTILE INTEREST.

One of the first, if not the first store in town, was kept by Joseph Clapp, Jr. He commenced trading in 1792, in his house, nearly opposite the store of A. J. Lyman, on Main street. He was a brother of Dea. Thaddeus, son of Capt. Joseph, and grandson of Maj. Jonathan Clapp. He married Susannah, daughter of Timothy Lyman, of Chester. On the day of his marriage, Mr. Lyman said to him, "You are now going to trading; the maxim of the world seems to be, trade so that you can live by it; my advice is, trade so that you can die by it." If this advice were followed by all, whether engaged in mercantile or other employments, there would be much less reason for distrust in business circles, and greater stability in financial affairs.

In a few years Mr. Clapp erected a building for his accommodation, on the top of "meeting-house hill," where the hotel now stands. He was for a time one of the most influential men in town, and filled the office of town clerk longer than any other man, with one exception.

After his retirement, Bohan Clark kept a store in the same building. He was an enterprising man, and accumulated considerable property. For a time he owned and carried on the grist-mill, and also a share in the saw-mill, lately owned by Edwin S. Janes, which was torn down to give place to the cotton mill of S. Williston & Co. He finally went to Northampton and engaged in business.

He was succeeded in business by Eldad Smith, a young man of good moral and religious principles. He was one of those who were engaged in the establishment of the Sabbath school here. About 1821 he sold out and removed to Granby. After this the business was carried on successively by Baxter Burnell and William R. Gillett.

In 1841 the building was sold out and removed to Union street, where it was remodeled and enlarged, and since that time it has been used as the seminary boarding house.

In the early part of the present century, Asahel Janes, and after him Obadiah Janes, kept store in the house formerly occupied by Capt. Ferry, near the hotel. He, in common with his cotemporaries, kept and sold ardent spirits. This traffic was not considered disreputable in those days. It was countenanced by men of the highest standing in society. Public opinion had not been aroused to a sense of the baleful effects of spirituous liquors upon the whole man, physical, intellectual, and moral.

The universality of the use of these liquors in those days astonishes us. Although the people of this town were not uncommonly addicted to their use, yet, then, if a person went to a raising, a husking, or an apple paring; if he chanced to step into a neighbor's as a hog was being weighed, or anything unusual being done; at every quilting party, wedding, or even funeral; in short, everywhere that neighbors or friends met together, they were treated with spirits in some of its various forms. We have reliable authority for saying that at that time not less than twenty-five hogsheads of spirituous liquors were retailed annually in the town. In one year there was manufactured more than a hundred barrels of cider brandy. There were four distilleries here and as many as six cider mills. Surely no one familiar with these facts, can say with sincerity, that there is as much liquor drank now as then though not so openly.

We rejoice to see that a deeper interest is at present

manifested in this important subject, and that more earnest efforts are being put forth by the friends of temperance, to stem the increasing tide which has threatened, or we may say, even now does threaten to engulf us in its desolating waves. In order that these efforts may have their fullest degree of efficiency they must be as persistent and unremitted as this depraved appetite of man is constant. We shall have great hope of the glorious temperance cause when every little child is taught to avoid the evil, to pass by it, to turn from it and pass away; when they are led to the altar, like the Carthagenian Hannibal, and made to swear eternal enmity to King Alcohol; when they are taught by precept and example at every step of their progress from infancy to manhood, to shun it entirely, in all its forms, as they would the venomous cobra or the deadly upas tree. Till then we almost despair of any radical and lasting reform.

The building in which a store was kept by Obadiah Janes, was afterwards occupied by Ebenezer Ferry, who commenced store-keeping in 1843, at which time he received the appointment of postmaster. In 1850 his increasing business demanded more ample accommodations, and he accordingly hired a room in Knight's block, which had just been erected. He has occupied this place until his recent retirement, when he was succeeded by F. H. Putnam. Capt. Ferry is a native of the town, and has been in public business considerable; was town clerk for twenty-one years, and has been justice of the peace for a long time.

In 1835, Mr. Williston opened a store near his residence, more particularly for the purpose of paying his employees, although he sold goods to other people. For several years H. G. Knight was employed by Mr. Williston as a clerk. In this capacity he so won the esteem and confidence of his employer, that, at the age of eighteen, and after, he was entrusted with the purchase of goods, and soon came to manage nearly all the affairs of the firm, whose sales were considerable, in some years amounting to $40,000. In 1842 or '3, Mr. Williston sold out to Mr. Knight and E. L. Snow, who carried on the business two years, when the copartnership was dissolved and the business closed, and the building used several years as a warehouse; but on the transfer of the button works in 1848, it was moved to a location near the factory.

At this time, the firm of John H. Wells & Co. was formed. With Mr. Wells were connected, as special partners, Mr. Williston and Mr. Knight. Mr. Williston retained an interest in the concern till 1858, when he sold out and Odel Gregory became a partner, and the business was conducted by the firm of Gregory & Wells, until the death of Mr. Gregory, since which time it has been carried on under the old name of John H. Wells & Co.

In 1830, Luther Clapp erected a building just north of Manhan river, on the banks of the old Farmington canal. This he used for a store ten years, when he sold out to Harris Bartholomew, who retained the place till 1850, when he removed to Northampton.

In May, 1855, John Mayher opened a tin shop in the place. That business had been started here by Miletus Parsons, but he died shortly after, and was succeeded by S. W. Lee, Jr., who however continued here only one year. Since Mr. Mayher came here his business has steadily increased, so that it is now perhaps larger than that of any other similar establishment in the county, if we except the trade in stoves. He is now engaged in the manufacture of an improved oil can, patented by himself, and which has given good satisfaction wherever used. He gives constant employment to nine hands, and does quite a large business in the course of a year.

The mercantile business of the town is now done by R. M. & J. E. Lambie, dry goods ; Winslow & Ward, drug store ; John H. Wells & Co., and A. J. Lyman, dealers in dry goods, groceries, hardware, crockery, etc.; F. H. Putnam, dealer in groceries, medicines, books, stationery, etc.; John Mayher, plumber and stove dealer ; L. Preston, D. Machol, and J. E. Miller, merchant tailors; Rust & Marsh, dry goods, ready made clothing, groceries, crockery, etc.; C. W. Langdon, Arlow Hannum & Son, and Stratton & Parsons, groceries and provisions; C. H. Chapman, watchmaker and dealer in jewelry; B. W. Hutchinson, boots and shoes ; Hawkins & Kent, millinery and dress goods ; Misses Thrall, millinery ; D. S. Jepson, flour, meal, and feed ; R. E. Strong, toys, confectionery, etc.

MILLS, TRADES, &c.

First and foremost among these is the saw and planing mill, until recently owned and carried on by the late L. P. Lyman. His business in lumber has been probably quite as extensive as that of any other man in the county. His lumber has, most of it, been used in the town, yet such has been the demand for building materials within the last few years, that large quantities, both of lumber and brick, have been brought from other places. His mill stands on the Manhan, near the center of the town. Upon the opposite side of the river, and drawing their supply of water from the same pond, stands a tannery belonging to Horatio Shoals, and a flouring mill owned by Edward Clapp and the heirs of L. P. Lyman, where a good business is carried on.

With this mill is connected quite a history.

"In 1676-7, Northampton gave Samuel Bartlett liberty to set up a corn mill upon Manhan river, below the cart-way, on the falls of the river." He probably soon after built it. In 1705, he gave it to his son, Joseph Bartlett, who took charge of it till his death, which occurred in 1755.' He, having no children, gave it to his nephew, Jonathan Clapp, who lived with him. He also carried it on till his death, when it fell into the hands of two of his three sons, Jonathan and Joseph. About 1810, the former sold out his interest in the concern to Joseph Clapp, Jr., the store-keeper. The latter gave his interest to his sons. On the failure of Joseph Clapp, Jr., Bohan Clark came into possession of his share, and carried it on in company with the other partners, until about the year 1815, when Ahira Lyman purchased his interest. It was owned by Messrs. Clapp and Lyman, till their death, when it fell into the hands of their sons, who have since owned it. It has been rebuilt twice since its erection by Samuel Bartlett. It will be noticed as somewhat remarkable, that for more than one hundred and seventy-five years the ownership of the mill has continued in the same family. In the aggregate, an immense amount of grain has there been ground.

In 1803, a company consisting of Jonathan Strong and brother, Jonathan Bartlett, John Phelps, and Simeon Clark, built a saw-mill on Saw-mill brook, about a mile above its junction with the Manhan. For fifty years, without much interruption, it was worked, but in the spring of 1854, during the time of the famous "Nebraska Deluge," the dam was carried off, and has never been rebuilt. The saw-mill standing where the cotton mill of S. Williston & Co. now stands, built in 1797 by Bohan Clark, has before been alluded to. There have been two saw-mills on Broad brook, in the south-east part of the town, one of which still stands, owned by Benjamin Strong. The other was owned by Stephen Hendrick.

Caleb Loud of Loudville, owns a saw-mill in the north-west part of the town, and near it is situated the grist-mill of Franklin Strong, at which a good flouring business is done. Another saw-mill in the south part of the town is owned by Alva Coleman.

There are three meat markets in town at present, owned by W. H. Avery, E. H. Ludden and A. S. Ludden. The following facts appear from the census of 1865. The number of pounds of dressed beef, 102,251. The number of feet of lumber prepared for market is 915,000. The two flouring mills report the number of bushels of grain ground during the year at 25,000. There are two master builders in this place, E. R. Bosworth and T. J. Pomeroy, who employ 39 hands. The number of buildings erected in the year previous to the taking of the census was twenty, whose value was $107,000. This, however, does not include all the buildings put up in the place during the year, nor nearly all the men thus employed.

The business of steam and gas fitting is carried on by Geo. L. Manchester, dealer in steam, gas and water pipe, and fittings of all descriptions. Mr. Manchester settled here about three years since, and the large amount of building which has been done has given him a good business.

Oliver N. Clark and Ralph Smith are established here as carriage makers; Erwin Robinson, and L. O. Toogood, as painters and glaziers; Edward R. Smith as a photographic artist; George P. Shoals and Wm. E. Topliff as masons; J. E. Janes, as market gardener; R. Goldenblum, Dennis Lyman, T. Colgan, and G. Friday, as shoemakers; and James Connell, Edward Reed, and Wm. Parlow as blacksmiths. Wm. R. Searle has recently opened coffin warerooms, and is prepared to furnish anything which is needed from an undertaker.

There are three livery stables in town, kept by D. S. Jepson, Hiram Knapp, and Edwin E. Janes.

CHAPTER VII.

PHYSICIANS, CASUALTIES, CEMETERIES.

PHYSICIANS.

The number of physicians who have practised in Easthampton, is not large. Rarely, if ever, until within a few years, has there been more than one at a time. The population was small, and general health has prevailed.

Dr. David Phelps commenced the practice of medicine here about 1780, and remained six or eight years.

Dr. Hophni Clapp, a native of Southampton, studied medicine with Dr. Woodbridge of that town, and came here about 1790. His medical reputation was good. He interested himself considerably in town affairs, and was honored with several offices of trust. His life was spent in Easthampton.

Doctors Hall, Munson, and Edson, were here for a short time.

Dr. Zalmon Mallory, a native of Montgomery, settled here not far from 1815. He acquired an extensive practice, and, during his stay in the town which lasted twenty years, he endeared himself to the people, by his sympathy and considerate attention. In his feelings, he was uncommonly ardent, but they seldom led him to the performance of injudicious acts. He took a warm interest in the common schools, and was for some years a member of the general committee. He was always very upright, and cherished a high regard for the institutions of religion, so much so that, unless circumstances absolutely demanded it, he would not call upon patients during the services of the Sabbath. But it was not until 1831 that he professed an interest in Christ. From that time he was a very active and exemplary member of the church. In 1835 he removed to Michigan, where he died.

In the same year, Dr. Atherton Clark commenced the practice of medicine here. For many years he was the only physician in the place, and won the esteem and confidence of the community. He was considered a very successful practitioner, and enjoyed a high reputation among the members of the medical fraternity, for a thorough knowledge of the science.

Dr. Solomon Chapman, Dr. Addison S. Peck, Dr. Thomas Henderson, and Dr. Barker, each practiced medicine here for some time. Dr. Chapman died here, and the others removed from the place.

The physicians at present residing here are Dr. F. C. Greene, and Drs. Winslow & Ward.

Dr. Greene has enjoyed considerable opportunity for the practice of surgery, as well as medicine, having been connected, for a short time, with our army in the Mexican war, and more recently as army surgeon, he served in Virginia and Louisiana, during a period of two years.

Dr. Winslow, who has for several years enjoyed a wide practice in our community, has recently united with himself Dr. Ward, who was for a time employed in the army as surgeon of the 38th Mass. Reg. He was afterwards appointed to the position of Medical Inspector, on the staff of Gen. Sheridan, in which capacity he served during the Shenandoah and closing Virginia campaigns.

Dr. Winslow was formerly engaged in practice in Enfield, where he was succeeded by Dr. Ward.

R. D. Brown, Thomas Bolton, A. E. Strong, R. E. Strong, and H. S. Bascom, have practised dentistry here, of whom the last two now reside in the place.

CASUALTIES.

One morning in January, 1780, Samuel Coleman and Ezekiel Wood went out hunting deer. By some means, they became separated, and, as it was a foggy day, objects could not be distinctly seen at a great distance. Presently, Mr. Coleman noticed a rustling in the bushes not far from him, and supposing it to have been made by a deer, he fired at once. His feelings, when he discovered that his shot had taken deadly effect in the body of his friend, can better be imagined than described. This event filled with mourning the heart of his young wife, thus suddenly bereft of her husband, and of an aged widowed mother, and sent a thrill of sorrow through the hearts of a sympathizing community.

About the year 1790, Lucas, a little son of Lt. Asahel Clark was drowned, near where the cotton mill of Williston & Co. now stands.

In April, 1798, Bohan Clark undertook to transport a lot of timber, from this place to South Hadley canal, on the river, for the frame of a store which he was about to erect. The water in the Connecticut was high, and he determined to avail himself of the opportunity thus presented. The timber was lying at his saw-mill near where the cotton mill of S. Williston & Co. now stands. The water of the Connecticut backed up to his mill, and on this he rafted his timber, and set out with his brothers Eleazer and Asahel, together with two others, intending to guide the raft into the canal at the falls. But somehow, as they approached the canal, an unexpected current seized it, and hurried it forward to the dam, which had been thrown across the river to turn the water into the canal. The raft was carried over the dam uninjured, save by the detachment of a small portion, on which Mr. Bohan Clark was standing. That remained upon the dam, and he instantly seized a spike pole, and held by main strength against the force of the current. The other persons escaped the first fall unharmed, but below a fearful fate awaited them, unless they could get to the shore. A large natural fall lay about two miles below, near where the dam now stands. Mr. Eleazer Clark was one of those cool, self-possessed persons, whom no danger can deprive of judgment, who always distinguish themselves in great emergencies. To get the raft to land seemed to him simply impossible. He therefore determined to construct hastily a smaller raft, on which they might reach the shore. This being accomplished, three of them stepped on it, and then the fourth, Mr. Asahel Clark. His weight caused the raft to sink about eighteen inches. Almost in despair he stepped back, and commenced the construction of a small raft for himself. When it was finished, he stepped upon it; but he had approached so near the fall, that all his efforts were of no avail, and he was carried over the fall. For some time he survived the shock, but before any boat could come to his assistance, he became exhausted and sank. The other three, by great exertion succeeded in reaching the shore in safety. Mr. Eleazer Clark, after seeing that efforts to save his brother Asahel were useless, turned his attention to the rescue of his brother Bohan, who was upon the dam, and for two terrible hours had maintained his position against the current, while no one came to his aid. By the well-directed efforts of his brother and others, he was removed from his perilous position, and brought to shore. The very instant he left the detached portion of the raft, it was carried over the dam. The body of Mr. Asahel Clark, was not recovered for some time. He was 31 years old at the time of his death, and left a wife and two small children.

In January, 1797, Moses Gouch and Joseph Davis were felling trees in a lot of woodland, on Manhan river, back of the house formerly owned by Solomon Ferry. While thus engaged, Mr. Gouch was struck by a limb of a falling tree, and instantly killed.

In January, 1817, while Eleazer Ring was superintending the moving of a building, he received injuries which resulted in his death. The floor of the house had been taken up, and while in the building, he missed his foothold and fell, and before the team could be stopped it had passed over his body. He survived but a few hours.

In the year 1819, the owner of a piece of woodland, on the west side of Mt. Tom, not far from its southern extremity, had cut sixty cords of wood or more, and had piled it up compactly, intending to slide it down the mountain, in a road which he had prepared for the purpose. Of course an event of this kind, not being of common occurrence, called together quite a company, especially of boys, who after the wood had been slid down, went up to the top of the mountain, and commenced rolling down stones, before all had reached the summit. Cecil Brown, a boy of fourteen years of age, was the last to come up. One of his companions, who was a little in advance of him, called out to them to desist, saying thoughtlessly, "you have killed Cecil." In a short time they returned, and found him lying down, and apparently dead, he having received a blow from a stone which fractured his skull. He however, revived, was trepanned, and lived many years; but so severe was the shock that his mental powers were very much impaired, and his intellect permanently enfeebled.

About the year 1826, Elijah Alvord, who lived in the east part of the town, started from home to walk to Northampton, on the Connecticut river, which was then frozen over. As he did not return at the time expected by his friends, search was instituted and it was found that he had broken through the ice and was drowned.

In 1831, Samuel Knowlton, who lived in the east part of the town, was kicked by a horse which was feeding in the street, and received injuries in consequence of which he died.

On the night of Dec. 15, 1835, an event occurred which filled the community with sadness. It was the death of Ocran Clapp, who perished in the snow. He had attended a public meeting that evening in the town hall, which stood near the recent site of the First Church. During the evening a snow storm of unusual violence had sprung up, attended with a severe and increasing degree of cold. He lived on the Northampton road where Ansel Bartlett now does, and, on leaving the hall, instead of taking the road home, by mistake he took the one leading east towards Pascommuck. He passed on until he arrived near where the cotton mill of S. Williston & Co. now stands, when probably having discovered his mistake, he turned about. When he had gone back some distance, he turned off into the lot, probably intending to cross to his residence, which would save considerable. Instead, however, of turning towards home, he turned directly opposite, passed on Broad brook, where it appeared he had broken through the ice, and passed on the plain beyond. His age, sixty-five years, his bewilderment, and the wetting which he received at the brook, together rendered him unable to endure the storm and intense cold of the night. He was found dead the next morning, at no great distance from the brook. The light which he carried was observed by several, but no one thought strange of it, since people were then returning from the meeting. Some effort was made to find him on the evening before, but it was finally thought that he might have gone into some house, and search was given up.

On the 11th of Oct. 1835, Ahira Lyman met with an accident which occasioned his death. He lived in the west part of the town, where Elijah Lyman now resides. He was chopping wood in a ravine, at some distance from his house, and while thus engaged, accidentally struck the top of his foot with the axe, which passed through the foot, and the sole of the shoe, and struck the log. He called for help but no one heard his cries, and he was compelled to crawl on his hands and knees nearly home. The great loss of blood weakened him very much, but the wound was skillfully dressed, and for a number of days there seemed to be a reasonable prospect of his recovery. The case however at length seemed to take an unfavorable turn. He sank very rapidly, and died on the 1st of Nov. 1835.

In 1836, Charles Brown, adopted son of Obadiah Clark, was run over by a cart and killed.

In November of the same year, Bela Hannum was found dead in the Manhan meadow, somewhere between the residence of Edwin Hannum and that of John Bosworth of Southampton.

In May, 1842, a little child of Augustus Clapp was drowned in Manhan river, while returning from school, having accidentally fallen from the bridge which he was crossing.

On the 1st of August, 1844, Ichabod Wright, who resided on Park Hill, was found dead in his field, lying beside a small brook, with his face in the water. There were no means by which the singular circumstances of his death could be satisfactorily accounted for. This event was deeply felt by all, since he was highly esteemed as a Christian man.

In the summer of 1845, Stephen Wood, Jr. was killed by falling from a load of hay upon a pitchfork.

In May, 1848, the wife of Justus Lyman died in consequence of injuries received from a fall.

In April, 1857, the community experienced a severe loss in the death of Dea. Ithamar Clark. While attempting to remove a heavy rock from its bed, a chain broke, and the rock, falling back, struck a lever, throwing it violently against his head. His injuries were so great, that he survived only three days. At the time of his death, he was one of the deacons of the church, in which capacity he had acted for 24 years. He was a person of uncommonly sound judgment, unflinching integrity, and very conscientious. He early espoused the cause of temperance, and was always one of its firmest supporters. His attainments in piety were rare. He had drank deeply of the cup of affliction, and was ever ready, with a warm and generous sympathy, to comfort those who were called to mourning. A blow so unexpected filled the hearts of his family and friends with sadness, and left a void in the church which was deeply felt.

August 15, 1857, as Eli Taylor, a boy about fourteen years of age, was returning from his work, he was obliged to cross the railroad track, and in his haste or forgetfulness, attempted to cross while the cars were approaching with unusual speed. Just as he was in the act of jumping from the track, as it appeared, he was struck by the engine, and instantly killed.

In December, 1858, Alvan Upson, a boy employed in

the button factory of Williston, Knight & Co., met with a severe, and as it proved, a fatal accident. While in the wheel-room, his foot accidentally slipped and became entangled in the gearing connected with the water wheel, and was torn or crushed entirely off. The leg was amputated twice before the arteries could be taken up, but it was skillfully dressed, and the hope was entertained that he would recover with only the loss of a limb. On the second or third day, however, it commenced to bleed, and no surgical skill could save him.

On the 6th of June, 1859, a little daughter of Lewis S. Clark was so severely burned, in consequence of the taking fire of her clothes, that she died.

In the month of October, 1859, while the cotton mill of S. Williston was in process of erection, Issachar Ford, a carpenter employed upon the mill, received a fatal injury by the accidental falling of a stick of timber. He survived only eleven hours. He had but recently removed to the place. The blow fell suddenly and heavily upon his family, who were thus deprived of husband and father, and awakened sorrow throughout the community.

In September, 1864, H. Bodisco Chapman, whose home was here, was killed on the New Haven and Northampton railroad, in the town of Southwick. He was baggage master, but was at that time acting conductor of an excursion train. Having occasion to pass over the top of a car, while doing so, he was struck by a bridge which they were passing, and, as is supposed, instantly killed.

The recent death of Edward I. Allen, a student of Williston Seminary, by drowning, is too fresh in the minds of all, to need rehearsal. The sad event occurred while he was bathing, unaccompanied by any one. It occasioned a feeling of deep sadness in the Institution with which he was connected, and left his class to mourn the loss of one of their most promising members.

L. P. Lyman, who died Aug. 7, 1865, received an injury on his head, by the falling of a stick of timber at the raising of a house, which hastened, if it did not wholly cause his death.

Jan. 27, 1865, the death of a little child of Rev. Mr. Jackson was caused by tipping a cup of scalding water into its bosom.

On the 21st of April, 1866, William Whiting, a colored man, was struck by lightning, while on his way home from his place of labor. He was passing a large maple tree at the instant of the discharge, and a portion of the charge left the tree and entered his body, to all appearance killing him instantly. He left a wife to mourn his loss. He had been in the place but a short time, having come from Washington about a month before his death.

The town has not been wholly, though to a great degree, exempt from scenes of murderous violence.

In 1780, Elisha Brown was killed by a person named Norton, in a fit of ungoverned passion, near the present location of the factories. A few years later, an Indian woman was killed just below the grist-mill, as it was supposed by her husband.

These are believed to have been the only events of the kind, until 1865, when Jacob Kretz, a saloon keeper, received wounds resulting in his death, from a party of drunken persons, who forced an entrance into his house in the night, for the purpose of procuring liquor.

When this chapter of casualties was commenced, we were not aware that there were so many instances of this kind; but one after another has come to our knowledge, and perhaps even now the list is not complete. It is instructive, as teaching us the dangers to which we are exposed, and the great uncertainty of life. Surely death has all ways, as well as all seasons, for his own.

"Verily 'his time there's none can tell,' nor yet his manner. He wearies out one with old age, and drags down another by disease. He surprises one in the labors of the field, and bewilders another in the highway he has oftenest frequented, and lures him to the dreary waste to sink unattended and alone."

This record extends over a period of eighty-six years. How many of those who now inhabit this town, who walk its streets, carry on its business, and cultivate its fields, whose faces are seen and whose voices are heard in our public places, or how many of those who will come after us, will, within a similar period, be called away by a sudden and violent death, is to us all unknown. Equally uncertain is it, to whom the dread messenger will come. "Let our souls be shielded in the faith of Christ, and our hopes folded around the throne of eternal mercy. Then will we grapple with death, and though we fall, we shall conquer the conqueror, and then lay off our armor, and rest forever in the bosom of our God and our Father."

CEMETERIES.

The first burial place in Easthampton, was in Nashawannuck, and many of the early settlers in that part of the town were buried there; but many years have passed since then, and they are nearly forgotten; now but few can point to the place where they lie. It has been supposed that the place could not be identified; but there are a few who still remember the graves of their ancestors. The burial place is on an elevation, in a field belonging to Augustus Clapp, and about fifteen rods south-west from his house.

Would it not be well for those of the present day, to rescue these ancient cemeteries from oblivion, and by enclosing them, and erecting a plain and simple, but suitable monument, to show to posterity the last resting place of those daring, hardy ones, who braved the toils and dangers attendant upon the early settlement of our country?

Since that time, there have been three burial places occupied. The one first used in the center of the town, was opposite the place where Williston Seminary now stands. The land was originally owned by Benjamin Lyman, son of one of the purchasers of School meadow, and was probably given by him to the town for a burying ground. One of his children was the first person deposited there.

It is more than a hundred years since then, and, as the fathers and mothers of the town passed away one by one, here was their dust committed to earth, to rest until the resurrection morn. But the march of improvement disposed the present generation to devote it to other purposes. Hence, in the summer of 1865, the remains were removed to the grave-yard at present in use.

Another burial ground is in Pascommuck. It was given by Eliakim Clark, and the first one buried there was a child of Jonathan Janes, in the year 1775.

The other cemetery, situated about half a mile south of the churches, on the east side of Main street, was located in 1846. Mrs. Eunice S. Lyman, wife of Daniel F. Lyman, was the first person buried there. The lot originally contained four and one-half acres. Since then it has been enlarged once, and it is proposed to enlarge it still further. Since it was first occupied, many have been laid to rest within its limits.

Within these silent cities of the dead, are a multitude of all ages, of every condition in life, from the aged man of hoary hairs, to the infant of a few days; the bride just entering upon her new duties, with fondest hopes and anticipations; the strong man of business, cut down in the midst of life and health; those who have lingered long on the verge of the grave; merry laughing childhood, and youth, buoyant with life and happiness; all have been summoned by the messenger of death, and consigned to these silent tombs, there to await the sound of the arch-angel's trumpet, at the dawn of the eternal morning. And, as we gaze on the spot where they rest from their labors, may we learn the impressive lesson, that since death comes alike to all without distinction of age, rank, or condition, we ought to live in a state of constant preparation to obey its summons.

CHAPTER VIII.

MISCELLANIES.

THE LIBRARY ASSOCIATION.

The earliest records of this society have not been preserved. Hence we have no means of determining the precise date of its formation. It is presumed to have been as early as the year 1792. About thirty persons became stockholders by the payment of two dollars. Their meetings for the transaction of business, and the exchange of books, were held at the house of some member. Rev. Payson Williston, was, for thirty-five years, its efficient librarian. He performed in the aggregate a large amount of labor for the society, whose prosperity he regarded as of great importance. This association continued as a separate organization, through a period of fifty years, at the end of which time, it was united with the Youth's Library Association, a society which was formed in 1828. The object of this society, as stated in its constitution, was to excite in the minds of the youth a thirst for knowledge, to exalt and refine their intellectual and moral characters, by giving them access to such books as are of a moral tendency. Its members paid a fee of one dollar for membership, and an annual tax of twenty-five cents. Jan. 10, 1840, by a concurrent vote of the two societies, they were united under the name of the Easthampton Social Library Association.

In 1844, the library was moved to the town hall, where the members met quarterly for business and the drawing of books. In 1865, the constitution was revised, and it was provided that any person, not a stockholder, by the payment of fifty cents annually, could be allowed to take out books. The library was then removed to the store of L. Preston, who for several years took charge of it. We are sorry to say that very little interest is now felt in it.

Should the town establish a public library, as is contemplated, this of course would supersede the necessity for the continuation of the Library Association.

A choice collection of standard literature ought to be within reach of the people of the town. A library of reliable, substantial works, liberally sustained, and thoroughly read, would be of incalculable benefit, in correcting and cultivating the taste, and in improving the morals of the young. The books should of course be wisely selected, and every effort made to induce young men to devote their leisure time to reading, rather than to spend it in places of public resort, which are the schools of a type of morality, at least questionable.

PUBLIC HOUSES.

The first public house within the limits of Easthampton, was kept by Joseph Bartlett. It stood where stands the house formerly occupied by Dea. Thaddeus Clapp, a few rods north of Manhan river. Mr. Bartlett was licensed in 1727, and for nearly twenty years he kept an open house for the public. It was quite a noted place in those days, and one of much resort. When there was preaching in the neighborhood, as there often was, it was at his house. Undoubtedly, many times, that eminent man of God, Rev. Jonathan Edwards, D. D., proclaimed there those truths and those doctrines for which he was distinguished, and which were so wonderfully blessed in the conversion of thousands. A large part of the town belonged to his parish, and it is a fact not generally known that that great revival in 1734 commenced in Pascommuck—a revival which, in its progress and development, became the wonder of many in this country and in Great Britain.

Probably about 1750, Major Jonathan Clapp, a nephew of landlord Bartlett, commenced to keep tavern where Ansel Bartlett now resides. The soldiers from Southampton met here as they were about to start for Bunker Hill, in the days of the Revolution. Travelers passing between Connecticut and Vermont usually passed through this town, and quite frequently spent the night with Major Clapp. He continued in his business till his death, which occurred in 1782. He was a man of influence in the community, and many present residents of the town trace their genealogy back to him. He was a very shrewd business manager, and knew how to turn everything to good account. A story is told of him which illustrates this trait of character.

Probably about the year 1760, what was long known as "The Great Crust," took place. A body of snow, some four feet in depth, fell, and immediately on its surface eight inches of hail, and then a slight rain, which froze and formed a solid crust. The fences, as if by magic, had disappeared. The roads were all blocked up so that there was no communication with market. On the morning after the crust was formed, he took out his horse upon it, and saw that it bore him up. In a very short time he was mounted and on his way to Hatfield, where he purchased a drove of cattle, and on the next morning he was on his way to Boston, where he arrived in safety, the crust having borne him all the way. His drove was the first to enter the city after the fall of snow, and consequently he received a high price for his beef. The trip occupied a little more than a week, and he cleared £100 or $333.

After his death, his son Jonathan opened a tavern, in a house which he built, across the road from his father's old stand.

In 1793, Capt. Joseph, another son of Major Clapp, opened his house for the accommodation of good travelers, at the old stand of landlord Bartlett, where he continued to cater to the public until his death in 1797. He was succeeded by his son Luther, who for a period of fourteen years entertained the traveling public. Most of the travel from Hartford and New Haven to the north would pass through the town, and consequently he received a liberal patronage.

After him, his place was satisfactorily filled by his brother, Dea. Thaddeus. Persons whose business required them to pass this way, often became so much attached to him, on account of his affability and the good fare which his table afforded, that after his sign was taken down, and his house closed, whenever they had occasion to remain here, they insisted on stopping with him. Thus for a period of nearly or quite a hundred years, the only public house in town was kept by members of the same family, in succeeding generations.

After they had left it, for some time the town was without any hotel. The establishment of Williston Seminary here, in 1841, seemed to call for some place where strangers might be accommodated. Mr. Williston, therefore, erected the building at present in use for that purpose. Mr. Luther Clapp was the first landlord. Since he left it there have been frequent changes, no less than seven men having filled the place. It is now owned by the

Nashawannuck Manufacturing Co. A large addition, three stories in height, has recently been erected, and other improvements in the house and grounds have been made. It was closed for a time during these changes, but not long since it was re-opened to the public, and is now styled the Union House, of which George M. Fillibrowne is at present the landlord.

POST OFFICE.

Since the establishment of a post office in town in 1821, there have been seven post-masters. The following are their names, and the year of their appointment:—

Baxter Burnell,	1821.
Wm. R. Gillett,	1823.
Thaddeus Clapp,	1828.
J. Emerson Lyman,	1840.
Thaddeus Clapp,	1841.
Luther Clapp,	1843.
Ebenezer Ferry,	1843.
J. H. Bardwell,	1861.

The first two post-masters kept the office in a store which stood where the hotel now does. Dea. Thaddeus Clapp kept it in his tavern. Capt. Ferry kept it for the first few years in his store, in the house formerly occupied by him, but for the last fifteen years or more, it has been in Knight's block. When Dea. Clapp had the care of the office, its yearly avails were about $75.00. In 1860 they were about $650.00. Now, on the old plan of paying a commission to postmasters instead of a salary, the avails of the post office would be $1,500 or more. The number of letters mailed during the year 1860 was 32,133. The present rate is over 100,000 yearly, together with a corresponding amount of printed matter.

POPULATION.

When the district was incorporated, its population was small, being then only about 400. Since that time there has been an almost constant, though until recently not rapid, increase. Only once was there a diminution in the number of inhabitants, from the taking of one census to that of another. Between 1830 and 1840 there was a decrease of 28. The table shows the population at each census.

1790, 457; 1800, 586; 1810, 660; 1820, 712; 1830, 745; 1840, 717; 1850, 1,348; 1860, 1,928; 1865, 2,869. The present number of inhabitants is one more than four times the number twenty-five years since. The gain in that time has been 2,152. It was during the interval between 1840 and '50, that the manufacturing interest of the place took its rise. Since that time, the material growth of the town has been very rapid. Indeed, we think it doubtful whether any other town in the country can exhibit a similar increase in any period of its history.

INTERNAL REVENUE.

The law enacted by Congress to provide internal revenue to meet the demands of the government, took effect Sept. 1, 1862, from which date the first tax was assessed, though at that time there was no Income Tax. This contained the names of 32 persons and firms from Easthampton.

There were 23 Licenses issued at that time.

There were 8 Retail Dealers' Licenses.

There were 4 Manufacturers' Licenses.

First Income Tax, May 1, 1863.

64 names of persons and firms from Easthampton.

32 Licenses were issued.

9 Retail Dealers.
8 Manufacturers.
29 Incomes assessed, amounting to $188,410.
24 Carriages and Wagons, valued at $75 and upwards.

Second Income Tax, May 1, 1864.

68 names of persons and firms from Easthampton.
41 Licenses.
12 Retail Dealers.
9 Manufacturers.
28 Incomes, amounting to $255,129.
26 Carriages and Wagons, valued at $75 and upwards.

Third Income Tax, May 1, 1865.

127 names of individuals and firms from Easthampton.
89 Licenses.
20 Retail Dealers.
14 Manufacturers.
79 Incomes, amounting to $419,607.
63 Carriages and Wagons, valued at $50 and upwards.
53 Gold Watches taxed.

Fourth Income Tax, May 1, 1866.

169 names of individuals and firms from Easthampton.
75 Licenses.
66 Carriages and Wagons, valued at $50 and upwards.
67 Gold Watches.
93 Incomes, amounting to $340,539.
13 Manufacturers.
18 Retail Dealers.

The returns since May 1 of the current year, are incomplete. The number of licenses to retail dealers, manufacturers, and others, is not all in yet.

Total Manufacturer's Tax, for the year ending April 30, 1866, $100,919 32.

These figures, kindly furnished us by the Assistant Assessor, indicate very clearly the increase of business in the town during the period which they cover, the numbers, in some cases, having more than trebled.

The first Assistant Assessor was Levi Parsons, the exact date of whose appointment we have been unable to find. A re-appointment of his bears date Sept. 30, 1863. Failing health forbade him longer to continue in the office, and LaFayette Clapp was appointed in his place, by President Johnson, June 6, 1865. He has continued in the office to the present time, having been re-appointed by the Secretary of the Treasury, June 14, 1866. On the 14th of June, 1865, Mr. Clapp was appointed Inspector of Distilled Spirits, and on the 4th of October, 1865, Inspector of Tobacco, Snuff, and Cigars. Both these gentlemen have discharged the duties of their office with fidelity and acceptance.

TOWN OFFICERS.

Selectmen.

1785—Stephen Wright, Capt. P. Clark, Eleazer Hannum.
1786—Stephen Wright, Capt. P. Clark, Eleazer Hannum.
1787—Benjamin Lyman, Elijah Wright, Eleazer Hannum.
1788—Philip Clark, Elijah Wright, Eleazer Hannum.
1789—Philip Clark, Elijah Wright, Eleazer Hannum.
1790—Lemuel Lyman, Joel Parsons, Noah Janes.
1791—Lemuel Lyman, Joel Parsons, Noah Janes.
1792—Lemuel Lyman, Joel Parsons, Aaron Clapp, jr.
1793—Lemuel Lyman, Joel Parsons, Oliver Clark.
1794—Eleazer Hannum, Noah Janes, Oliver Clark.
1795—Elijah Wright, Lemuel Lyman, Joel Parsons.
1796—Eleazer Wright, Noah Janes, Oliver Clark.
1797—Elijah Wright, Lemuel Lyman, Joseph Clapp, jr.

1798—Noah Janes, Lemuel Lyman, Joel Parsons.
1799—David Lyman, Levi Clapp, Joel Parsons.
1800—Oliver Clark, Levi Clapp, Solomon Lyman.
1801—Oliver Clark, Joel Parsons, Solomon Lyman.
1802—Oliver Clark, Uriel Clark, Levi Clapp.
1803—Oliver Clark, Uriel Clark, Levi Clapp.
1804—Oliver Clark, Solomon Lyman, Justus Lyman.
1805—Oliver Clark, Solomon Lyman, Jonathan Janes, jr.
1806—Thaddeus Clapp, Sol. Lyman, Jonathan Janes, jr.
1807—Thaddeus Clapp, Oliver Clark, Justus Lyman.
1808—Jonathan Janes, jr., Oliver Clark, Justus Lyman.
1809—John Hannum, Thaddeus Parsons, Justus Lyman.
1810—John Hannum, Jonathan Janes, jr., Justus Lyman.
1811—John Hannum, Thaddeus Parsons, Justus Lyman.
1812—John Hannum, Thaddeus Clapp, Justus Lyman.
1813—Solomon Lyman, Thad. Parsons, Justus Lyman.
1814—John Hannum, Solomon Ferry, Justus Lyman.
1815—John Hannum, Solmon Ferry, Justus Lyman.
1816—John Hannum, Solomon Ferry, Justus Lyman.
1817—John Hannum, John Ludden, Seth Janes.
1818—John Hannum, John Ludden, Jonathan Janes.
1819—John Hannum, John Ludden, Jonathan Janes.
1820—John Hannum, John Ludden, Jonathan Janes.
1821—John Hannum, John Ludden, Jonathan Janes.
1822—John Ludden, Ocran Clapp, Julius Clark.
1823—John Ludden, Ocran Clapp, Julius Clark.
1824—John Ludden, John Hannum, Luther Clark.
1825—John Ludden, John Hannum, Luther Clark.
1826—John Ludden, John Hannum, Luther Clark.
1827—Levi Clapp, John Hannum, Luther Clark.
1828—Levi Clapp, John Hannum, Luther Clark.
1829—Levi Clapp, John Hannum, Luther Clark.
1830—John Ludden, John Hannum, Luke Janes.
1831—John Ludden, Daniel Lyman, Luke Janes.

1832—John Ludden, Daniel Lyman, Luke Janes.
1833—John Hannum, Levi Clapp, Luke Janes.
1834—Luther Clark, Levi Clapp, John Ludden.
1835—Luther Clark, Jason Janes, John Ludden.
1836—Luther Clark, Jason Janes, John Ludden.
1837—Luther Clark, Jason Janes, John Ludden.
1838—Luke Janes, E. W. Hannum, John Ludden.
1839—L. P. Lyman, E. W. Hannum, Luther Clark.
1840—L. P. Lyman, E. W. Hannum, Luther Clark.
1841—E. W. Hannum, Augustus Clapp, Lorenzo Clapp.
1842—E. W. Hannum, Zenas Clark, Solomon Alvord.
1843—E. W. Hannum, Zenas Clark, Solomon Alvord.
1844—Theodore Clapp, Zenas Clark, Solomon Alvord.
1845—E. W. Hannum, Luther Clark, Theodore Clapp.
1846—E. W. Hannum, Luther Clark, Solomon Alvord.
1847—E. W. Hannum, Luther Clark, Solomon Alvord.
1848—Lemuel P. Lyman, Luther Clark, Solomon Alvord.
1849—Lemuel P. Lyman, Luther Clark, Solomon Alvord.
1850—E. Ferry, Luke Janes, Solomon Alvord.
1851—E. Ferry, Luke Janes, H. G. Knight.
1852—E. W. Hannum, Luke Janes, H. G. Knight.
1853—E. W. Hannum, E. Ferry, Luther Clark.
1854—J. H. Lyman, E. Ferry, Luke Janes.
1855—L. F. Clapp, Q. P. Lyman, Ransloe Daniels.
1856—L. F. Clapp, Joseph Parsons, Solomon Alvord.
1857—E. W. Hannum, Joseph Parsons, L. P. Lyman.
1858—Alanson Clark, L. F. Clapp, E. H. Sawyer.
1859—Alanson Clark, L. F. Clapp, Levi Parsons.
1860—Alanson Clark, L. F. Clapp, Levi Parsons.
1861—Alanson Clark, Lewis S. Clark, Levi Parsons.
1862—Lewis S. Clark, Alanson Clark, Seth Warner, Lauren D. Lyman, Lewis Clapp.
1863—Lauren D. Lyman, Seth Warner, E. S. Janes.
1864—Lauren D. Lyman, E. S. Janes, E. A. Hubbard.

1865—Edwin S. Janes, Lewis S. Clark, Joel Bassett.
1866—Joel L. Bassett, Ansel B. Lyman, Lewis S. Clark.

Town Clerks.

1785—David Lyman,	3 years.
1788—Jonathan Clapp,	2 years.
1790—Joseph Clapp, jr.	
1797—Hophni Clapp,	6 years.
1803—Obadiah Janes, 2d.	
1804—Joseph Clapp, jr.,	11 years.
1808—Obadiah Janes, 2d,	9 years.
1816—Isaac Clapp.	
1817—Zalmon Mallory.	
1821—Isaac Clapp,	2 years.
1822—Zalmon Mallory,	11 years.
1829—Samuel Wright,	5 years.
1834—Ebenezer Ferry.	
1841—Edwin Hannum,	1 year.
1842—Ebenezer Ferry,	20 years.
1855—Lucius Preston,	9 years.
1864—George S. Clark,	1 year.
1865—Charles B. Johnson.	

School Committees.

1826—Samuel Williston, Zalmon Mallory, Samuel Wright, Solomon Clapp, Luther Clark, jr.
1827—Rev. P. Williston, Zalmon Mallory, Zenas Clark.
1828—Rev. P. Williston, Theo. Wright, Ezekiel White.
1829—Rev. P. Williston, Ezekiel White, Luther Clark, jr.
1830—Rev. P. Williston, Zenas Clark, Chandler Ludden.
1831—Samuel Wright, Luther Clapp, Sidney Ferry.
1832—Sidney Ferry, Emelius Clapp, Gideon Matthews.
1833—Sam'l Williston, Wm. Hannum, Gideon Matthews.
1834—Rev. P. Williston, Rev. Wm. Bement, Sidney Ferry.

1835—Sam'l Williston, Sidney Ferry, Samuel Wright.
1836—Sam'l Williston, Sam'l Wright, Rev. Wm. Bement.
1837—Rev. Wm. Bement, Sam'l Williston, Sidney Ferry.
1838—Rev. Wm. Bement, Edwin Hannum, Ather'n Clark.
1839—Rev. Wm. Bement, Ather'n Clark, Edwin Hannum.
1840—Edwin Hannum, Rev. Luther Wright, Luther Clark, jr.
1841—Rev. Wm. Bement, Rev. Luther Wright, Edwin Hannum.
1842—Edwin Hannum, Rev. Wm. Bement, E. Monroe Wright.
1843—Rev. Wm. Bement, Edwin Hannum, E. Monroe Wright.
1844—Eleazer Coleman, Rev. Solomon Lyman, Edwin Hannum.
1845—Edwin Hannum, Rev. Solomon Lyman, Eleazer Coleman.
1846—David N. Smith, C. Mattoon Alvord, Edwin Hannum.
1847—Edwin Hannum, Rev. Wm. Bement, C. Mattoon Alvord.
1848—Rev. Wm. Bement, D. M. Kimball, Edwin Hannum.
1849—LaFayette Clapp, Jas. H. Lyman, Edwin Hannum.
1850—L. F. Clapp, Jas. H. Lyman, Rev. Luther Wright.
1851—Rev. R. S. Stone, L. F. Clapp, Rev. Luther Wright.
1852—Rev. R. S. Stone, Rev. Luther Wright, James H. Lyman.
1853—E. A. Hubbard, Rev. A. M. Colton, Rev. Hervey Smith.
1854—Rev. A. M. Colton, E. A. Hubbard, Rev. Hervey Smith.
1855—Rev. Hervey Smith, Edward Hitchcock, jr., L. F. Clapp.
1856—Lewis S. Clark, Lauren D. Lyman, Rev. Luther Wright.

1857—Rev. Luther Wright, Lewis S. Clark, Lauren D. Lyman.

1858—E. A. Hubbard, Rev. A. M. Colton, Rev. Luther Wright.

1859—E. A. Hubbard, Rev. A. M. Colton, Rev. Luther Wright.

1860—E. A. Hubbard, Rev. Luther Wright, H. G. Knight.

1861—Rev. Luther Wright, H. G. Knight, E. A. Hubbard.

1862—H. G. Knight, E. A. Hubbard, Rev. Luther Wright.

1863—E. A. Hubbard, Rev. Luther Wright, H. G. Knight.

1864—Rev. Luther Wright, H. G. Knight, E. A. Hubbard.

1865—H. G. Knight, Russell M. Wright, Rev. Samuel Jackson.

1866—Russell M. Wright, H. G. Knight, Seth Warner.

REPRESENTATIVES IN GENERAL COURT.

1810—Dea. T. Clapp.
1811—Dea. T. Clapp.
1812—Dea. T. Clapp.
1813—P. Nichols.
1814—P. Nichols.
1815—Capt. L. Lyman.
1816—Capt. L. Lyman.
1817—John Hannum.
1818—John Hannum.
1819—Ahira Lyman.
1820—Dea. T. Clapp.
1821—Dea. T. Clapp.
1822—Dea. T. Clapp.
1823—Dea. T. Clapp.
1824—Dea. T. Clapp.
1825—Ahira Lyman.
1826—John Ludden.
1827—John Ludden.
1828—John Ludden.
1829—John Ludden.
1830—Ocran Clapp.
1831—Luther Clark.
1832—John Ludden.
1833—Jason Janes.
1834—Jason Janes.
1835—Luther Clark, jr.
1836—Luther Clark, jr.
1837—Luther Clark, jr.
1839—John Ludden.
1840—Samuel Williston.
1843—E. W. Hannum.
1844—E. M. Wright.
1845—Zenas Clark.
1848—H. Bartholomew.
1849—J. Wright, 2d.
1850—John Wright.

1851—H. G. Knight.
1852—H. G. Knight.
1853—Lemuel P. Lyman.
1854—Seth Warner.
1859—LaFayette Clapp.
1862—Eli A. Hubbard.
1865—E. H. Sawyer.

The following persons have served as Justices of the Peace, the first of whom was commissioned in 1810 :

Thaddeus Clapp.
John Ludden.
Luther Clark, jr.
Samuel Williston.
Ebenezer Ferry.
William N. Clapp.
Charles B. Johnson.
Lemuel P. Lyman.
Luther Wright, jr.
E. Waldo Lyman.
Addison S. Peck.
Horatio G. Knight.
Levi Parsons.
George S. Clark.

QUARTER CENTURY RETROSPECT.

It will be interesting, at this time, to review the progress of the town during the last quarter of a century. Let us glance back to the year 1840, and imagine ourselves passing through its streets, of which there were, then laid out, only those now known as Bridge, Main, Park, Union, and Pleasant Streets. Entering the town from the north, after we had crossed the bridge over Manhan river, we should come first to the house then occupied by L. P. Lyman, and the saw-mill opposite. Where now stands the hotel, would have been seen the building, since remodeled, and used, at present, as the Seminary Boarding House. On the left stood the house now owned by E. R. Bosworth, then occupied by Rev. Wm. Bement, pastor of the church, and also, a little farther on, the house formerly occupied by Rev. Luther Wright, but recently removed to give place to the First Church. On our right, we should pass the houses now owned by Capt. Miller and Dr. J. W. Winslow, in the latter of which lived Dr.

Atherton Clark. A little farther on, we should see, on our left, the First Church edifice, then newly erected, and, on our right, the old Town Hall, now used as a dwelling house by Edmund W. Clark. Passing the burying ground then in use, we should come to the blacksmith shop of Almon Chapman, standing where Knight's block now does, while directly opposite, on the present grounds belonging to Williston Seminary, was his residence. A little farther on was the house of Elihu Lyman, where F. H. Pomeroy now lives, and, nearly opposite, the dwelling of Isaac Clapp. The next house which we should pass would be that of Dea. Solomon Lyman, and still further south that of Jeremiah Lyman, where his son Ansel B. now lives. Beyond this there were none, until we reach that now occupied by Mrs. Janes. If, instead of Main, we had taken Park street, the only residence would have been that of Mr. Williston, on the site of his present one, while across the way stood his store. If, instead of this, we had taken Union street, though it could hardly have been called a street, we should have found only one house, until we reached the Pascommuck road running along the base of Mt. Tom. This stood at a little distance across the brook, where is now the Factory village. Soon after this the Seminary Boarding House and that of Almon Chapman were moved to their present location, and, for several years, these three were the only houses in that part of the town.

Now, retracing our steps, let us pass the church, and take the road leading to Pascommuck, now called Pleasant street. On the corner, was the house now owned by Horace Matthews, and the one next to it was then occupied by Joel Parsons, Senior, since, however, owned by Lewis Ferry. Opposite to this stood that now owned by Lowell E. Janes. A little farther on we should reach the dwellings of Joel Parsons, Jr., and of Spencer Janes, where now E. S. Janes resides. Four other houses, those of Solomon Ferry, Theodore Lyman, and one a little to the west of his, together with one standing not far from where Arlow Hannum now lives, would bring us to the saw-mill of Spencer Janes, where now the cotton mill of S. Williston & Co. stands.

Now let any one, bearing these statements in mind, pass, either in reality or imagination, along these streets and others since laid out, and observe the changes which a quarter century has witnessed, and he would be strikingly impressed with the progress of the town during that period.

Then the only church in the place stood where it has since, until its recent removal. Luther Clapp kept store, between the river and canal, where L. F. Clapp now lives, and Mr. Williston had a store across the road from his residence. Almon Chapman carried on the blacksmith's business, as we have said, where Knight's block now stands, and Samuel Wright supplied customers with fresh meat. The lumber and flouring business was in much the same hands as now, though in extent it has increased greatly.

Since then, the Hotel, Parsonage adjoining, High School, Town Hall, and Knight's block of stores, and others in the place, have been put up. Williston Seminary has been established, and, with all its buildings, stands an ornament to the place. Two new churches have been organized, and church edifices erected. The extensive manufacturing interest, with its mills and villages, has all sprung up, and a portion of the town where was then but one house has become its most populous part. Many fine private residences have been erected, and everywhere we meet with marked evidences of growth. The railroad and telegraph lines, and the lighting of the village with gas, are other great improvements.

Then the population was 717. In May last it was 2,869. With this advance in business and population, has come a still greater advance in the valuation of property in the center.

In 1848, H. G. Knight purchased a lot of land lying on Union street, and embracing that now occupied by the Payson Church, and the residences of H. J. Bly, D. S. Jepson, John Mayher, and Mrs. Miletus Parsons, two acres in all, paying therefor $200 per acre. In 1865 a quarter acre lot adjoining this was sold for little more than $1000, or more than twenty times as much as was paid for the same amount eighteen years ago by Mr. Knight.

Another, and a sad evidence of the growth of the town, is to be seen in its cemetery. Laid out in 1846, the surface of the original portion is already dotted all over with marble slabs, which mark the last resting place of some loved one; while one addition and another have been called for, as new families have removed hither. One by one they have been brought to tenant this city of the dead. One by one shall we who remain pass away, and our bodies be committed to earth. The time of our departure we know not, for "of the day and the hour knoweth no man." But, sooner or later, to each one it will come, and happy will it be for us if we be found in readiness, and watching for the summons.

MISCELLANIES.

Among the records of the old militia company of this town, under date of October 2d, 1827, after the usual record of the doings of the company, we find the following entry, which is very suggestive and interesting: "At the above training, the company voted unanimously that the officers should, on all occasions, abolish the practice of treating with ardent spirits. A noble resolution—let it be kept sacred." This may be considered to mark an era in the history of temperance reform. Hitherto, custom had required that the officers, at their election, and on other occasions, should treat the men under their command. It was a practice entirely pernicious in its workings, and without any natural foundation, though, in those times and before, it was carried into almost every department of life. Men at length began to awaken to a consideration of the wide spread evils of such a course, and hence arose the temperance reformation, a work most beneficent in its results and calculated to secure to society incalculable blessings, if wisely persisted in. Of late years, however, an apathy on the subject seems to have taken possession of the minds of the friends of this reform, while its enemies are ever on the alert. Many professedly temperance men have fallen into the old habit of using and treating with the lighter liquors, as cider and domestic wines, and, as it seems to us, from precisely this source, has originated something of the alarming increase of intemperance in our communities. If we would withstand successfully this vice, whose desolating effects are but too plainly visible all around us, we must come up to the high ground of the old temperance reform, and persistently maintain its principle of total abstinence from everything that can intoxicate.

An incident of interest, which has come to our notice, though known perhaps to some, is deserving of mention here. Rev. Luther Wright, on the day on which he reached the grand climacteric of life, (his sixty-third birth-day,) ate his thanksgiving dinner in the room in which he was born, with his father and mother beside him. A case of this kind, where so many circumstances of interest cluster around a single event, rarely happens in any community.

It is a fact, perhaps not generally known, that the elm which stands in the center of the park, where the original church edifice stood, is planted directly beneath the place occupied by the old pulpit. It was set out by Luther Wright, father of the one previously mentioned, not long after the building was taken down.

The elm which stands nearly in front of the recent site of the First Church, was set out when quite small, by Zadok Danks, then nearly ninety years of age, who obtained it somewhere in the Manhan meadows. This is an interesting circumstance, and it would not be inappropriate if the name of this public benefactor should be borne up in the tree which he planted.

On the 14th of January, 1856, Luther Wright and wife celebrated the sixtieth anniversary of their marriage. It was an occasion of unusual interest, and such an one as rarely occurs. Rev. Payson Williston who married them, and who survived the celebration only about two weeks, was present, as were also four others, who attended the marriage sixty years before.

DEED OF SCHOOL MEADOW.

It may be interesting to many to know that the deed of School Meadow, which the town of Northampton gave to Stephen Wright and Benjamin Lyman, is still in existence. Such is its connection with the early settlement of the town, as to justify the insertion of some portion of it here, particularly that part relating to the boundaries of the tract. It reads as follows:—

"To all persons to whom these presents shall come, Greeting:— Know ye that we, John Stoddard, Ebenezer Pomroy, and Timothy Dwight, all of Northampton, in the County of Hampshire, in His

Majesty's province of Massachusetts Bay, in New England, a committee appointed by the town of Northampton to make sale of the sequestered land that lies on both sides of the Manhand river, between the county road across said river, above Bartlett's mills, and the Pomroy land, for and in consideration of the sum of sixteen hundred and twenty-five pounds, in bills of Public Credit, Old Tenor, secured to the town of Northampton by Dea. Stephen Wright and Benjamin Lyman, both of Northampton, aforesaid, the receipt of which is hereby acknowledged, and in said capacity we, the said Stoddard, Pomroy, and Dwight, are fully contented and satisfied, do therefore acquit said Stephen Wright and Benjamin Lyman, of all dues and demands whatsoever, on account of said land excepting Public Security, have, in the capacity aforesaid, given, granted, bargained, and sold, and by these presents do freely, fully, and absolutely give, grant, bargain, sell, convey, and confirm to them, the said Stephen Wright and Benjamin Lyman, and to their heirs and assigns forever, (viz.), one half to be his, the said Stephen Wright, to his heirs and assigns forever, and the other half to the said Benjamin Lyman, his heirs and assigns forever, the whole of the above mentioned tract or parcel of sequestered land which is more particularly bounded as follows, (viz.);—It is land that was formerly sequestered by the town for the school, bounded eastwardly by the place where Filer's Brook formerly emptied itself into Manhand river, and from thence it extends up Manhand river on both sides, as far westwardly as to land laid out to Thomas Dewey, on the north side of the river, now belonging to Eldad Pomroy. The upland on the north side of the meadow is to extend westwardly as far as to the home lot of Caleb Pomroy, deceased, bounded southerly by the brow of the hill on the south side of School Meadow, and northerly by the highway running west on the south side of the Long Division, extending westerly to Pomroy's land, which highway is to remain from Filer's Brook, aforesaid, which, (or Saw-mill brook as it is sometimes called,) as it now runs to the top of the hill on the level land or plain, and then to turn northerly to the highway on the south side of the Long Division."

The remaining portion is very similar to what may be found in any deed at the present day, and contains no points of special interest.

This instrument was executed on the 28th of May, 1745, in the presence of Preserved Clapp, Nathaniel Dwight, and Timothy Dwight, Jr.

CHAPTER IX.

THE CIVIL WAR.

To write the history of the town, as it relates to the civil war so recently closed, is a duty both joyous and sad. We rejoice to speak of the patriotism of our citizens, of the heroic achievements and self sacrificing spirit of those who participated in it, and of the part, which we as a community, had in defending the institutions transmitted to us by our fathers; but we are saddened, as we record the names and deeds and deaths of some of our noblest young men, who were possessed of sterling character, patriotic devotion, high and consistent regard for truth and right, and steadfast purpose to serve their day and generation wherever Providence might call them. Doubtless He, who directs the affairs of men to the accomplishment of His own grand designs, knew how they could best subserve the object of their existence; but as we recall their many virtues, and the promise of usefulness they gave, we cannot but mourn their early death. It is, moreover, a difficult task to weigh out equal justice to every one. Our desire is to deal fairly by all, and to speak of the service performed by each in different fields, without instituting any invidious comparison as to the relative value or merit of those services.

In the time of the Revolutionary War, of Shay's rebellion, and of the war of 1812, our population was not numerous, and, though our part was faithfully performed, the number of men called for was by no means large, while, in the Revolutionary war only, was much real military service performed. Only a few can now remember the drafts then made upon us. None of our inhabitants engaged in the Mexican war, a war which was the result of a measure obnoxious to the greater part of the people. Fifty years of undisturbed peace had rendered us unfamiliar with the arts and paraphernalia of war. In the earlier portion of this period, there were, it is true, military companies and parade days; but these had entirely ceased, and few of those in early life had ever seen a militia soldier. We thought that our nation stood strong. Though other nations might be rent by civil commotions or foreign war, we hoped that we might be exempt. But the time was approaching when war, in its numberless forms of horror, was to become to us an actual reality.

It would be needless to detail the events preceding and attendant upon the election of President Lincoln in the autumn of 1860, the secret plots of traitors, and the temporizing of President Buchanan during the remainder of his administration, the attempts upon the life of the President-elect, his inauguration, and the vigorous though conciliatory policy which he adopted, the development of secret treachery into open revolt in the attack upon Fort Sumter, and the subsequent grand uprising of the people. All these events are still fresh in our memories, and will there remain fixed. We remember well the days of eager expectancy and intense excitement which succeeded the issue of the call for 75,000 volunteers, when the nation's capital seemed to be surrounded by its enemies, and all open communication with it suspended.

We did not then think that we were entering upon a

protracted struggle of four long, terrible years. We did not think that the call for men was to be so oft repeated. We did not know that the remorseless hand of war was to enter almost every home, and that from many of these homes some loved one was to fall a sacrifice. In wisdom the future was hidden from our sight. A short time passed, and it became apparent that 75,000 men, in three months, could not quell a rebellion, which was from day to day assuming more gigantic proportions. Accordingly, a call was issued by the President for the enlistment of men for a three years' term.

The first to respond to this call were James H. Clark, who joined the second Mass. regiment, commanded by Col. Gordon, Roland Williston, who had but recently come into the place, and perhaps was not credited to the town, and who also joined the second Mass. regiment, Gustavus W. Peabody, Edward Graves, and Henry L. Ferry, who enlisted in the 10th regiment at the time of its formation. Henry L. Ferry was a member of the regiment about eighteen months, taking part in McClellan's peninsular campaign. He was at last discharged on account of poor health. At a subsequent period however, he joined the 31st Mass. regiment, and remained with them until they were mustered out. Gustavus W. Peabody retained his connection with the regiment so long as it continued in the service, and was with it in most of its battles, though absent a short time in consequence of a wound in the arm received at the battle of Salem Heights.

Albert S. Gove, Salmon H. Lyman, and Richard Goodsell, went to New York, and enlisted in a regiment known as the Anderson Zouaves. Of these three, the first mentioned went through the whole three years of his enlistment without a wound, although he was in many, if not all of the battles in which the army of the Potomac were engaged, up to the time of his discharge. For a portion of the time, he was engaged in detached service at the headquarters of Gen. Wheaton. Salmon H. Lyman, after serving about one year, was taken sick and died. Before his sickness he was with McClellan, on the Peninsula, and fought at the battle of Williamsburg.

These, hitherto named, enlisted in the early part of the year. The summer wore away, and the call came for more men. The 27th regiment was mustering at Springfield. Its ranks must be filled, and we must come forward to aid. Efforts were made to procure enlistments, and the following men from this town enrolled their names:—Thomas Bolton, Lafayette Clapp, Alvin W. Clark, George P. Clark, William P. Derby, Charles D. Fish, Sylvester S. Hooper, John H. Judd, Frederick P. Stone, Justus Lyman, Thaddeus Lyman. The last mentioned of these did not, however, long remain in the regiment, owing to a severe sickness which attacked him soon after going into camp.

These men joined Co. A, and were mustered into the service Sept. 20, 1861. They left Camp Reed, Nov. 2d, and went to Annapolis, Md., where they joined the forces gathering under Gen. Burnside. With his expedition they sailed, and assisted in the capture of Roanoke Island, Feb. 8, 1862, and afterwards in the battle and capture of Newbern. Of these just mentioned, William P. Derby was appointed to a position in the post office, which he retained during his period of enlistment. Lafayette Clapp was detailed for hospital service, and remained at Newbern, part of the time only with the regiment, until near the close of the war. The latter part of the time he was employed in connection with the Sanitary Commission and White Refugee Department. The others followed the fortunes of the regiment. For a long time they were required to do garrison and provost duty in and about Newbern, though on one occasion they engaged in an expedition to Goldsboro, and also at other times on difficult marches. They also shared in the defense of Little Washington, during a protracted siege of seventeen days,—a siege most gallantly and successfully sustained. In the summer of 1862 they received a considerable accession to their number, from those who volunteered, in response to a call of the President for 300,000 men.

Those who went from this place were William Bly, Henry Braman, Oliver A. Clark, George A. Hill, Lyman A. Howard, Elisha C. Lyman, Patrick Murphy, Ezra O. Spooner, Spencer C. Wood. To these may be added Henry Lyman, who although he was not counted on our quota, was a native of this town, and held the same place in the regard of the community which the others did. For about a year he performed faithfully the duties of a Christian soldier. In the summer of '63, he sickened and died at Newbern. Elisha C. Lyman, another of this number, joined Co. A, in which he already had a brother; but his military career, though heartily entered upon, was to be short. He died at Newbern, Dec. 26, 1862. Spencer C. Wood remained in the army but a short time, in consequence of sickness, which led him to obtain a discharge.

In the winter of 1863–'4, the regiment was transferred to the department of Gen. Butler in Eastern Virginia, and spent the winter at Norfolk and Portsmouth. In the spring, our men took part in the advance of Butler up the James. For several days they were engaged in fighting along the railroad between Richmond and Petersburg. On the 16th of May, while fighting at Drury's Bluff, many of the regiment, including the greater part of Co. A, were taken prisoners, having been surrounded by the enemy, whose movements were concealed by a dense fog. The following soldiers from this town were captured:—Thomas Bolton, Henry Braman, Alvan W. Clark, Oliver A. Clark, Sylvester S. Hooper, Lyman A. Howard, John H. Judd, Justus Lyman, Patrick Murphy, Edward Merrigan, Ezra O. Spooner, Frederick P. Stone. To this list of captured may be added the name of Rufus Robinson, who although at the time of his enlistment he was living in Southampton, and counted on their quota, yet had for a number of years previously resided in this town. He had joined the regiment only a short time before the advance up the Peninsula.

J. H. Judd, who had been promoted from sergeant to first lieutenant, was at the time in command of Co. A, and Justus Lyman, who had received a similar promotion and had been assigned to another company, were confined two weeks in Libby Prison, and then sent successively to Macon, S. C., Charleston, and Columbia, S. C., and Charlotte, N. C. On the 16th of February, 1865, after having been confined nine months, Lieut. Judd, in company with a few others, made his escape, and, after meeting with various adventures, reached a place of safety with a Union man, until the advance of Sherman about that time, brought relief. Lieut. Lyman was exchanged about the time of Lieut. Judd's escape. He retained his connection with the army until the close of the war, before which time he received a captain's commission.

The other prisoners were taken to Andersonville, which place they reached May 30. In this den of horrors they were confined, and endured, as long as life lasted, those sufferings and tortures which have stamped with infamy the rebel cause, and which for magnitude and enormity, stand almost unrivalled in the record of human atrocities. Of the number sent here, five died. Their names were as follows: Oliver A. Clark, Alvin W. Clark, Ezra O.

Spooner, Frederick P. Stone, Rufus Robinson. The others were released at last, and permitted to return home.

In the fall of 1861, after the men who had joined the 27th regiment had gone, enlistment rolls were opened to obtain men for Gen. Butler, who was then raising a regiment in the western part of the state. The following men enrolled their names, and went into camp at Pittsfield: Theodore E. Bartlett, Amasa Braman, Joseph U. Braman, Leonard Braman, William Bryant, Egbert I. Clapp, Martin S. Dodge, Albert H. Ford, Samuel D. Gould, Chauncey A. Hendrick, William Hickey, John Leavitt, Almon S. Ludden, James F. Mahar, William Newton, Wilbur H. Purdy, Henry V. Rich, Fordyce A. Rust, Charles S. Rust, Richard Wright.

Of these, A. S. Ludden, being unable to leave the state in consequence of sickness, was discharged. Theodore E. Bartlett and William H. Purdy were with the regiment only during the early part of its career. Richard Wright was discharged. Chauncey A. Hendrick was taken sick, and returned home, where he died shortly after his arrival. William Hickey was killed in battle at Camp Bisland. The others served out all, or nearly all, the three years.

F. A. Rust went as 1st Sergeant of Co. B, but was promoted to 1st Lieutenant, and transferred. Charles S. Rust went out as Sergt., was detailed as Quartermaster Sergt., and finally was appointed Quartermaster, with the rank of 1st Lieut. On the promotion of Lieut. Rust, Egbert I. Clapp was appointed Quartermaster Sergt., and before the expiration of his term of service received the commission of 2nd Lieut. M. S. Dodge, Orderly Sergt., was on detached service a part of the time at Gallop's Island.

The military history of the regiment may be said to be

that of the others. They went out with Gen. Butler, and were the first Union soldiers to enter New Orleans. For a time they were employed in garrisoning Fort Jackson. They were in the battle of Camp Bisland, took part in the march through the Teche country, and were engaged at Port Hudson during all the siege of that stronghold. After this they participated in the Red River campaign of Gen. Banks, during which they were engaged in the battles of Cane River, Pleasant Hill, Pine Bluff, Sabine Cross Roads, Bynam's Mills, Gov. Moore's Plantation, and Yellow Bayou.

This season their term of service expired, and of them the following re-enlisted and were allowed a furlough home:—William Bryant, Egbert I. Clapp, Martin S. Dodge, Albert H. Ford, John Leavitt, James F. Mahar, William Newton, Charles S. Rust, Samuel D. Gould, the last of whom was wounded at the battle of Pleasant Hill. In the fall of 1864, those who did not re-enlist came home, while those who did re-enlist remained till the close of the war. In the early part of 1865, they were ordered to Florida, and afterwards to Mobile, where they were stationed as provost guard until the regiment returned.

The summer of 1862 came, and with it a call for 300,000 more. The question of duty to country was coming more and more closely home to every man. A new regiment, the 37th, was being raised in this section, and a number entered it, though the men who volunteered at this time had the privilege of being assigned to any other regiment which they should elect. It was at this time that the men before mentioned as recruits for the 27th, enlisted. The others who volunteered were William Bartlett, Marshal Blythe, H. Bodisco Chapman, Charles H. Clark, David Fahey, Andrew J. Ferrell, Andrew J. Hill, Daniel Kane, Alpheus W. Parsons. Of this number, the last named was taken sick not long after entering the service, and was discharged. H. B. Chapman remained for a longer period, but was finally discharged. Chas. H. Clark was transferred to the Veteran Reserve Corps, where he served till the close of the war. Daniel Kane died the first winter out, while in camp at Falmouth. Only four, A. J. Ferrell, A. J. Hill, David Fahey, and Marshal Blythe, remained with the regiment till it was mustered out. The honorable course and hard service of the 37th are well known. They were with the Army of the Potomac most of the time, when not in the Shenandoah valley with Gen. Sheridan. The four named were in nearly, or quite, all the following battles, while some of the others were in the earlier ones :—

Fredericksburg, Salem Heights, Mary's Hill, Gettysburg, Mine Run, Wilderness, Spotsylvania, Coal Harbor, Petersburg, Fort Stevens, Charlestown, Opequan, Hatcher's Run, Fort Fisher, Petersburg, Saylor's Creek. The last two of these engagements were those fought in the final contest with the forces of Gen. Lee.

Scarcely had the call for three years' men been met, when a draft for 300,000 nine months' men was ordered. The quotas of the different towns in the state were made out, that of this town being about forty. The number was nearly twice as great as had gone on any previous occasion, and many who had heretofore shrank from the sacrifice, and hoped that the great conflict might pass without demanding their aid, now felt that the call of duty came to them. Efforts were made to procure enlistments so as to avoid the necessity of a draft. Public meetings were held for several successive evenings, until, at last, the requisite number had enrolled themselves. This was about September 1. They remained at their homes however, until the 1st of October, on which day they assembled at the depot, and took their departure for Camp Miller, Greenfield. Our men, together with those from Hatfield, Southampton, and Westhampton, constituted Company K, which was assigned to the left of the regiment.

The names of those from Easthampton, were as follows: 1st Lieut. Lewis Clapp, Commissary. Lewis S. Clark, Whitney F. Alvord, Lyman H. Bartlett, Clinton Bates, Frank L. Boehm, Charles L. Boehm George M. Clapp, William E. Clapp, Edmund W. Clark, Frederick C. Colton, Charles W. Dawes, Edward M. Ferry, S. Williston Graves, James T. Graves, Henry F. Gridley, Joseph K. Hull, Edwin E. Janes, Charles W. Johnson, John G. Keppel, Albert A. Lyman, Charles H. Lyman, Daniel W. Lyman, John W. Lyman, Samuel K. Matthews, Lucius E. Parsons, Herbert W. Pomeroy, William W. Poole, Stephen W. Pierce, Alfred S. Shaw, George W. Shaw, B. Milton Smith, William G. Taylor, Lorenzo D. Trask, Lewis P. Wait, Charles L. Webster, Enoch E. Wood, Newton Wood, Luther L. Wright,

The first member of the company, and indeed of the regiment, who died, was Lewis P. Wait, who was in camp but about two weeks, and died one month from his first day in camp. The attendance of the company at his funeral was an occasion of melancholy interest, and will not soon be forgotten. Another occasion of deep interest was that of the presentation, in behalf of the Sabbath Schools, of a pocket edition of the Testament and Psalms, to every man. On the 20th of November, they broke camp at Greenfield, and started for New York. Many of their friends met them at Northampton, where they stopped a few moments, and bade them a tearful, to some, a last farewell. They were a noble body of men, and left a void in our community more felt, because larger, than any which had been left before. Yet, men as noble, patriotic, and true, had gone before, and had been missed in our community—men whose sacrifice and risk were greater, from the longer term of service upon which they entered. Arriving at New York, they soon joined the forces of Gen. Banks, encamped on Long Island. On the 2d of December, they set sail for Ship Island arriving there the 13th, sailed up the Mississippi, and landed at Baton Rouge the 18th, where they spent nearly three months. Most of them participated in the first march to Port Hudson. On the 27th of March, they left Port Hudson for Brashear City, took part in the march of Gen. Banks through the Teche country, and were left at Barre's Landing to guard the post, while the main army went on to Alexandria. On its investment of Port Hudson, they were ordered to join the besieging forces, and marched to Berwick Bay, a distance of one hundred and twenty-six miles, in five days and two hours, and the last fifty-three miles in twenty-eight consecutive hours. Not long after they had rejoined the army they took part in the unsuccessful Sabbath assault on the enemy's works, June 14th. On this day, one of them, Daniel W. Lyman, lost his life by a ball from a rebel sharpshooter. They remained until the surrender of the place, July 8th, soon after which they started up the Mississippi on their return home, being the first regiment to sail up that river after its opening. They arrived at home on the 3d of August, and were mustered out the 14th. This notice of the doings of Co. K, is substantially the history of our thirty-eight men, and is given in this way to avoid repetition, though some, from sickness, did not participate in the active service of the campaign. Alfred S. Shaw was taken sick and did not go out with the regiment.

In the autumn of 1862, about the time of the enlistment of the 52d regiment, Alonzo S. King enlisted in the navy, and was assigned to the Henry Hudson, which was stationed off the coast of Florida. He remained a year, during which time he performed faithful service.

The following persons were members of the 1st Mass. cavalry:—Asa S. Strong, Frank Hoyt, John Kinloch, Edwin Fahey, William Dehill, James Newton, the latter of whom remained in the service only about two years. John Kinloch was taken prisoner twice, and the last time was confined at Salisbury for six months. Thomas O'Donnell enlisted in the winter of 1863–4, and joined this regiment and from this time was with the regiment in every battle which it fought till the war was over. Edwin Fahey was taken prisoner during the operations of the cavalry on the Weldon Railroad, and was sent to Andersonville, where he remained nine months.

Hugo Oberempt joined the 5th Connecticut regiment, June 5, 1861, was with Gen. Banks in the Shenandoah campaign, at both battles of Winchester, and Cedar Mountain, where he was taken prisoner and confined one month on Belle Isle. He was exchanged, and fought at Chancellorsville and Gettysburg. He was in the corps of General Hooker, which joined General Sherman, participating in the campaign from Chattanooga to Atlanta, at the battles of Resacca, Cassville, Lost Mountain, Kenesaw, Culp's Farm, and Peach Tree Creek, at which place he was wounded. He was then transferred to the corps of Topographical Engineers, in which capacity he accompanied Sherman in his grand march to Savannah, and afterwards in the campaign through the Carolinas, at the battles of Chesterfield, Averysboro, and Bentonsville. From Raleigh he marched to Washington, where he was in the grand review of Sherman's army.

Charles Braman was a member of the 34th Massachusetts regiment, which regiment performed good service in the campaigns in Virginia. He was with the regiment for two years.

Michael Fitzgerald joined the 82d New York regiment in the spring of 1864, and fought in the battles of the Wilderness, Spotsylvania, Coal Harbor, Deep Bottom, and White House Landing. He was wounded at the battle of Deep Bottom, August 14, 1864, and was discharged June 15, 1865.

Thomas Connolly enlisted in the navy August 27, 1862, and was assigned to the Monongahela, of Admiral Farragut's squadron, with which he was connected during the siege of Port Hudson. He was in the service two and one-half years.

At the same time with him John Quinn and John Donovan enlisted in the navy, the former being assigned to the Tennessee, and the latter to the Patapsco. They however remained only a year.

Justin W. Chapin was a member of a New York regiment. He was taken prisoner and confined in Andersonville seven months, but was finally released and returned home.

John G. Hennessey enlisted as a recruit in the 5th New Hampshire regiment, and served during the last year of the war in the "Army of the Potomac."

Charles Rensalear enlisted in the 54th Mass. regiment. In one battle he was wounded and taken prisoner, and nothing more was known of him till he was recognized by one of our citizens who was a fellow prisoner at Andersonville. He was then suffering from a wound in the breast, and died the next day after he was found out.

There are other men and probably more than have been called to our notice, who while they did not enlist from this place, and therefore did not count on our quota, are yet in some way connected with us, and whom we may claim as Easthampton soldiers.

Among these the name of Dr. F. C. Greene may, with propriety, find place, for, although he did not go directly from this place, he had lived here before and does now. He was with McClellan in the Peninsula campaign, and very nearly lost his life in the Chickahominy swamps. He was afterwards in Louisiana, with Gen. Banks, where he performed excellent service both in the hospital and on the field.

Augustus Clapp, son of Luther Clapp, was first a member of an Ohio three months' regiment, which was engaged in fighting guerrillas, and in guarding prisoners. He enlisted again as a member of the 3d regiment Ohio cavalry, in the autumn of 1862. In the early part of 1863, he was seized with the typhoid fever, and died in hospital at Nashville.

John Reagan enlisted Aug. 30, 1861, at Washington, D. C., in Co. B, 3d New York Cavalry, as farrier. He was discharged at Newbern, N. C., Sept. 30, 1862, from disability, brought on by exposure to dampness and cold at Poolesville, Md. He was in the Ball's Bluff fight, and his regiment were engaged in Western Virginia, in the early part of their service, whence they were sent to Newbern, N. C. Gen. Burnside had so high an appreciation of his services as farrier, that he wrote him a letter personally, urging him to come on again and take care of his horses.

Thomas Barbour enlisted December 22, 1863, and joined Co. B, 27th regiment. He served until June 26, 1865, and was in the following battles: Port Walthal Junction, Arrowfield Church, Before Petersburg, Petersburg Mine, Southwest Creek. He was captured in this last engagement, and paroled in Richmond, Va., May 26, 1865.

Charles and James S. Tencellent enlisted in the 10th Connecticut regiment. The latter served for a period of three years and was spared to return home, but the former lost his life in the battle of Olustee in Florida.

There were other soldiers whose names we have learned and give below, but respecting whom we have been able to collect very little information. Most of them were not natives or residents of the town, and were not known by individuals here. They performed no doubt excellent service and probably some of them lost their lives in the different battles in which they were engaged. Patrick McNamee, Michael Hafey, John Tencellent, Frank Thornton, Charles B. Hendrick, Joseph LaBiestens, John Howard, William Maffit, Dennis V. Champlin, 55th Mass. regiment; Martin Butler, Hugh Furfey, 6th Battery; Dexter Edwards, H. C. Hoffman, Louis Klein, 4th Mass. regiment; Henry Bedell, 4th Mass.; John Gerry, William Thomas, Pat. Walsh, Robert Fale, 15th Battery; James Nelson, 15th Battery; William Fogg, William B. Cloutman, Veteran Reserve Corps; Thomas Connor, 24th regiment; Richard Dane, James E. Sweatland, Henry Galloway, Louis J. Evans, Samuel Beattie, Edward Hogan, James Boardman, Navy; John Fluhine, 2d Heavy Artillery; Thomas J. Fisher, Joshua L. French, Daniel Ferguson, 10th Heavy Artillery; William G. Gage, 2d Mass. Cavalry; John Casey, Richard Davis, 2d Heavy Artillery; John Carson, 16th Unattached Artillery; James W. Crocker, 11th Infantry; Moses Graff, Edward Burns, 6th Battery; Pat. Welsh, Andrew Miller, John White, 2d Heavy Artillery; ——— Morey, William H. Turner, Daniel Crowin, Ralph Burnett, William Kyle.

Gilbert Sandy enlisted January 26, 1864, was taken prisoner and confined in Andersonville nine or ten months, and shared with other prisoners, and perhaps with some of those whose names are mentioned above, the horrors of that prison pen. Charles Morganweck was in the 27th Massachusetts regiment for a time.

The preceding record is supposed to contain the names of nearly all the soldiers furnished by the town. It contains all the names which have been placed upon the Rebellion Record, which include all the citizens of the place who served in the army. Our list also comprises many others whose names we have obtained from various sources.

About twenty-five of our citizens were represented in the army by substitutes. The names of nearly all of these, and perhaps of a few others, we have been unable to obtain.

It has been our purpose to make this record as complete and accurate as possible, though it has been a work of extreme difficulty. The whole number of men furnished or paid for by the town, is about 200, while the sum expended for bounties is $40,000.

The following brief notice of three sons of Joseph Alvord, now of Bement, Ill., but a native of Easthampton, and for many years a resident of it, will not be deemed out of place.

Lieut. Joseph C. Alvord, of Co. A, 21st Illinois regiment, enlisted at the beginning of the war, was in seven battles, and fell at the battle of Murfreesboro, Tennessee, December 30, 1862, while endeavoring to rally his men. One of his comrades in speaking of him, said: "he was an efficient officer, a noble man, and a gentleman in every sense of the word."

Oscar L. Alvord, enlisted in the 54th Illinois regiment, but not long after was taken sick in camp with the typhoid fever. He was taken home, but died a few days after reaching it.

Harrison M. Alvord, was a member of the 73d Illinois regiment, in which he served through the war, in the campaigns under Sherman. He passed through all his battles without a wound, though meeting with many narrow escapes.

Henry H. Smith, son of Rev. Hervey Smith of this town, was in Georgia, engaged in a printing office at the time of the secession of that State, soon after which he was ordered to leave the state or to join the rebel army. He immediately went to North Carolina, where he remained until Jefferson Davis ordered all aliens to leave the confederate states or to take the oath of allegiance. He at once made preparations to come north and succeeded in reaching Richmond, having eluded the watchfulness of vigilance committees of towns through which he passed. At Richmond he was on the point of taking the cars for the north, when he was arrested, taken before Gov. Letcher and others, examined, judged to be an enemy to the South, and thrown into prison. Here he was robbed of all his money, of his effects of every kind, and of all his clothing, save only a thin summer suit which he wore. To tell what he suffered there from hunger, and the cold of the following winter, as well as from the abuse of the prison officers, would be to rehearse the story of thousands who like him fell into their hands. While there he was repeatedly promised by a high official a release, and commission in the army, if he would swear to support the rebel government, but to all such propositions his reply was, no, *never, never.* From Richmond he was taken to Salisbury, N. C., and while there he was exchanged, after having been imprisoned twenty months. Immediately after his exchange he came home, and after some months of rest he obtained a situation in the Provost Marshal's office in New York. Here he remained for a time, but feeling a desire to do more for his country than he could there do, he enlisted in a company of light artillery which was formed in Jersey City. He went into camp in Washington, where after about five months drill he received a serious injury by the falling of his horse. The injury proving to be such as would incapacitate him for service in the army, after months of confinement and suffering, by the advice of his surgeon he sought and received an honorable discharge. His imprisonment and consequent sufferings were perhaps as much for his country as if he had been a soldier who had fallen into their hands, and he certainly is worthy of mention here in this connection.

It is fitting that we should here speak of the services of another of our country's defenders, to whom no community can lay claim with better right than this. We refer to Gen. George C. Strong. Born in Stockbridge, Vt., at an early age he was taken by his father to Chicago, and afterwards to Joliet, Ill., and by him on his death bed consigned to the care of A. L. Strong, of this town, who was his uncle. He received his academical education at Williston Seminary, and during this time displayed a remarkable predilection for a military career. In 1853, after indefatigable and for a long time almost fruitless exertions on the part of Mr. Strong, he was appointed to West Point. He graduated in 1857, standing third in his class, specially excelling all his classmates in the military exercises of the campus, and took the rank of commander of the battalion of cadets.

Lieut. Strong received his brevet in the Ordnance Department, and was for a while stationed at Selma, Ala., and afterwards at the Watervliet Arsenal in Troy, the command of which he received after Major Mordecai had proved untrue to his country. From thence he was called to the position of Chief of Ordnance to Gen. McDowell, and distinguished himself in the battle of Bull Run, by his cool courage and daring. Afterward he was attached to the staff of Gen. McClellan, with whom he remained until September, 1861, when upon application of Gen. Butler, he received the appointment of Assistant Adjutant General, with the rank of Major, and was transferred as Chief of Staff to Gen. Butler, and acting Chief of Ordnance. Major Strong's services were most valuable, and his labors incessant, in organizing the expedition to New Orleans, to the success of which he contributed not a little. Here his duties were so arduous, that his health gave way, and early in June, being seized with a fever of that country, he was obliged to come home to recruit. By September he had so far recovered his health as to be able to return to his duties. His activity of intellect could not be satisfied with the routine of office, and he obtained permission from Gen. Butler to head an expedition against a force of the enemy, under Gen. Jeff. Thompson, who were stationed at the village of Pontellatoula. After a closely contested action against a superior force, he succeeded in capturing the place, with a large amount of commissary stores which he burned, together with the railroad cars and public buildings. He brought off with him the spurs and sword of Gen. Thompson, which bore the inscription, "From the patriots of Memphis." When Gen. Butler was relieved from the command of the Department of the Gulf, Major Strong returned with him, and on his recommendation was promoted to Brigadier General of Volunteers, for his gallantry, courage, and efficiency. He remained attached to Gen. Butler's staff for a time, but at length finding that there was no prospect that he would be ordered into immediate service, although in a state of health which to many a man would have been suggestive only of a physican and a sick bed, he volunteered to go with Gen. Gillmore, to participate in the attack upon Charleston. To his brigade was assigned the post of honor in the attack on the batteries of Morris Island, upon which he was the first to land. His boots having become filled with water, he pulled them off and led the charge with only his stockings on. The batteries were gallantly carried, and the brigade afterwards received the congratulation of Gen. Gillmore, who said that it was the first instance during the war in which powerful batteries had been successfully assaulted by a column disembarked under a heavy artillery fire. He was placed in command of the troops on Morris Island, and given charge of the column which was to assault Fort Wagner. In this attack he received his death wound, while leading and inspiriting his men, who almost worshipped him for his daring, his kindness of heart, and his strict though impartial discipline. His injury produced lock-jaw from which he died on the morning of July 30th, 1863.

Some one has paid him the following noble tribute :—"Possessed of every endowment of head and heart, thoroughly trained by an education which had left both head and heart untrammelled to their noblest impulses, a loving husband, a doting father, the most genial of companions, the truest of friends, the bravest of soldiers, the accomplished officer, the daring leader, and withal a devout Christian, no more precious sacrifice has been laid on the altar of his country than George Crockett Strong."

If any apology is needed for giving this prominence to Gen. Strong, it is to be found in the fact that while he did not go from this place to the war, he is yet in some respect a son of Easthampton, and deserves mention among her sons. His military career being somewhat extended, could not well be sketched more briefly than it has been. While, as a military man, from his education, his genius, and his opportunities, his name may be said to stand at the head of those whom we claim as ours, there are others whose names are here recorded, who may justly be ranked as his peers in respect of patriotism, self-sacrificing devotion to the welfare of country, unswerving devotion to principle, and high moral worth.

To all who have enlisted from our midst, whether their names be found here or not, we owe, and desire to tender, our warmest gratitude. The separation from home and friends, the privations of the camp, the rigors of winter, and the feverish heat of a Southern summer, the weariness of the march by day and of picket by night, the dangers of the battle field, and the horrors of rebel dungeons, they have bravely borne. In the Shenandoah valley, they met the rebel ranks bent on invasion. With Burnside at Newbern, they conquered the foe, and set up the banner, which was there to float till the whole South was redeemed. Again, with Burnside at Fredericksburg, and with Hooker at Chancellorsville, they vainly strove to force the rebels from their position, and open the way to their capital. With McClellan at Antietam, and with Meade at Gettysburg, they met and rolled back the tide of invasion which was threatening to engulf us in its waves. With Butler, they redeemed the Crescent City, and vindicated the dishonored flag. With Banks at Port Hudson, they gloriously consummated the long struggle which unlocked the Father of Waters. With Strong at Wagner, they stormed the defences of that early citadel of rebellion. With Sherman from Chattanooga to Atlanta, from Atlanta to Savannah, from Savannah to Raleigh, they bore the flag in battle and in storm. With Butler along the James, and with Sheridan along the Shenandoah, they fought bravely and well. With Grant, they rallied and struggled through those long and bloody days in the

Wilderness. Step by step they drove back the rebel legions to their capital. There they planted themselves, and prepared for the final conflict. Weeks and months passed, the snows of winter fell and melted away. The final conflict, bloody and terrible, came at last, and victory was ours. Then, from Raleigh and Richmond they bore the triumphant banners, stained indeed with blood, and blackened with the smoke of the conflict, but all radiant with a new life. After four long years of waiting, of suffering and sacrifice, they brought the banners to Washington, that they, and their defenders, might receive the plaudits of a nation rescued from the assaults of treason, and consecrated anew to the principles of freedom and self-government.

At last they have returned home, have greeted once more the old familiar sights and faces, and have entered upon other employments than those of war. They have returned home, but, alas! not all. As they trod once more our streets, or gathered once more in our places of assembly, there were those who looked with tear-dimmed eyes on the war-worn group, for they missed the form of some loved one there, and they knew that beneath the cold clods of the earth, that form was lying. To some of them, indeed, the remains of those they loved were brought, and now repose among kindred and friends in the burial place of their native village. Others have found their last resting place along the banks of the Mississippi, or on the blood-stained fields of Virginia, while others still met death in Southern prisons, and now fill nameless graves. To one, death came almost before he had entered upon the active duties of a soldier's life. Some were permitted to enter upon their work, but were called away before it seemed half done; while others were spared almost to the completion of their term of service. The battle-field, the hospital, the Southern prison, each had its victims. They went forth full of life and hope, only to find death, —death without knowing that the sacrifice would avail, —death without witnessing the final success of the cause, —death "without the shout of victory, without the pride and glory of a return to receive the wreath and triumph of the conqueror."

The record of our dead in this war is a noble one and should be sacredly cherished as long as patriotism is honered or self-sacrifice calls forth our admiration and gratitude.

Salmon H. Lyman, son of Dennis Lyman, one of the first to volunteer, was the first to fall. In the first summer of the war, when the soldiers were rallying to the standard, he went to New York, joined the regiment known as the Anderson Zouaves, was home once on a furlough, spent one winter in camp, started out with Mc Clellan on his Peninsular campaign, and fought at the battle of Williamsburg, soon after which he was taken sick, and removed to New York, where he died. His remains were brought to his home, where they were buried with military honors, on the 18th of September, 1862.

Chauncey A. Hendrick was a member of Co. B., 31st Massachusetts regiment. He was with them for a time, but, after a period of sickness, it was thought best that he should return. With great difficulty, he was able to reach home, but survived only a few days.

Lewis P. Wait, son of Chester Wait, joined Co. K, 52d Massachusetts regiment, taking his life in his hand, as did the others, that he might serve his country. Little did he know, when he enlisted, how short his term of service would be. Fifteen days only, was he in camp. While at home on a furlough he was taken sick, and died after a sickness of some two weeks. His funeral, which was attended by his comrades, was an occasion of deep interest and solemnity, and will not soon be forgotten. In his death the company lost one who would have been faithful to his duties, whether those of camp and field, or the Christian duties of a soldier to those about him.

Daniel Kane, who had lived several years in Easthampton, though not a native of it, enlisted in the 37th regiment, in the summer of 1862. During the ensuing winter, while the army of the Potomac was encamped at Falmouth, he was seized with the typhoid fever, and no effort which was put forth could save him. He died, and was buried there.

Elisha C. Lyman, son of E. Waldo Lyman, was a member of Co. A, 27th regiment. He with other recruits, joined the regiment, of which his brother was already a member, in the summer of 1862. Not a long time was he spared to serve his country; for, upon him, as upon so many others, the hand of disease was laid, and consumed away his life, before he had performed much of that service for which he had volunteered. But the patriotic devotion was the same, and the sacrifice as costly, as if he had been spared to meet the enemy many times on the field of battle. His body was brought to the home from which he had so recently gone forth full of life and hope, and, amid sorrowing friends, it was committed to the earth.

Wm. Hickey, who had resided here but a short time, enlisted in Co. B, 31st Massachusetts regiment. He was a good soldier and a man of great bravery and endurance. At the battle of Camp Bisland, one of the first battles in which he was engaged, he was killed by a rebel bullet.

James H. Clark enlisted in the 2d Massachusetts regiment in the spring of 1861, soon after the breaking out of the war. He was with his brave regiment in nearly all their battles till his death. He was with Gen. Banks in his Shenandoah campaign, with McClellan at Antietam, and subsequently at Fredericksburg, Chancellorsville, and Gettysburg, not to speak of minor engagements. Through all these he passed unscathed. He had nearly completed the first half of his last year, and we hoped that as he had been spared so long, he might be permitted to return in safety. But this hope was not to be realized. The burning hand of fever was laid upon him, and he, who had faced death on so many fields, must, at last, bow before the touch of disease. His remains were brought to his home, and now repose among those of kindred and friends.

Roland Williston, who had been here but a short time when the war broke out, enlisted in the same regiment. He died from the effects of a wound received, if we mistake not, at Cedar Mountain.

Charles Tencellent, who was a member of the 7th Connecticut regiment, and who had resided here before the war, was in the disastrous battle at Olustee, Florida, and received wounds in consequence of which he died.

Henry Lyman, oldest son of Ahira Lyman, enlisted in the summer of 1862, and with others joined the 27th regiment, which was then in the field. For a little more than one year, he was spared to serve his country, and then he was called up higher. To his fidelity as a soldier and a Christian, his comrades could testify. Chaplain Woodworth said that he was one of those, upon whom he most relied for assistance in promoting the spiritual welfare of the soldiers. From the prayer meeting he was seldom absent, and there his voice was often heard in prayer and exhortation. Calmly and peacefully as the setting of the summer's sun he died,—died as only the Christian can die. Would that all the thousands whose death this war had caused, could have been sustained by a like precious faith.

Of the Easthampton soldiers who have died away from home, he was the fourth and last whose remains were brought home for interment. These all rest in honored graves in our cemetery, while of the others, many fill unknown graves, by the banks of the Mississippi, or in that thickly populated city of the dead at Andersonville. But to the ears of them all alike shall come that final trumpet, which shall summon forth the dead from their graves. Though we may not mark, and water with our tears, the sacred spot of their final repose, yet the recollection of them all shall be fragrant in our memories, and, to the last of life, we will not cease to honor their names.

Herbert W. Pomeroy, son of Julius Pomeroy, was a member of Co. K., 52d regiment. Like several previously mentioned, he was spared to complete only a small portion of his term of service. His disease was typhoid fever, the same which carried off so many of his regiment during the winter of 1862–3. He died at Plaquemine, while his company were stationed there. Of him the correspondent of the Gazette, from that regiment, said: "While on board the Illinois, he felt deeply the need of a Saviour, and we have reason to believe that he not only felt his need, but sought Christ and found him precious. The Sabbath before his death, he felt that he could not live, and expressed the hope that he was a Christian, and sent word home that he died trusting in Christ."

Daniel W. Lyman, son of Daniel F. Lyman, was a member of Co. K, 52d regiment, in which he was one of the first to enlist. Not from any fondness for the adventures and perils of war, nor from any momentary impulse, but from a deliberate conviction that to him the voice of country was the voice of God, was he led to offer himself, a sacrifice if need be, for his country's salvation. Upon a Christian young man not absolutely forbidden by some higher call of duty, he felt that the claims of country then were paramount. Influenced by such considerations, it is not too much to say, that, in the darkest hour, his purpose never wavered, nor did a regret for his course find place in his heart. To his faithful performance of the duties of a Christian soldier, many have borne ample testimony. His cordial, unwavering trust in God, in times of darkness and danger, though probably doubted by none, is best known to those who knew him intimately. To many whom he never saw, he was known by his letters from the regiment, which were published in the Hampshire Gazette. Most of the time during eight of the nine months for which he enlisted, he was permitted to share with his company their hardships and perils. But the New England home, to which he looked forward with longing, he was no more to behold. Sabbath morning, June 14, 1863, an attack on Port Hudson was ordered, and, though deprecating the selection of that day for the assault, he went forward without faltering. His regiment being engaged as skirmishers, he, with a few of his comrades, gained a position in a ravine somewhat in advance of the main line, and while here, very early in the engagement, a ball from a rebel sharpshooter struck him in his head, killing him instantly. It was his first and last battle. His was a sudden transition from the conflicts of earth, as we believe, to the peace of heaven. Capt. Bissell wrote thus in relation to him :—" Gentle hands placed him in his grave, and covered the earth over him near the spot where he fell, although obliged to wait till after dark, and to be exposed to a storm of rebel bullets. This tender tribute of affection is his monument, and, although his dust may not make the violets of his native hills, it will not be amiss, on the morning of the resurrection, that his body should arise from the spot, where the latest duties of his life were so faithfully concluded."

Were this the place for fraternal affection to give itself full expression, we might say more of his patriotism, of his fidelity to principle, of the promise of future usefulness which he gave, and of the sorrow which his early death occasioned. In a kindred sorrow, however, thousands of homes in our country, and many in our midst, have shared; and it is a sorrow better known by those who have been called to it, than expressed by any words of ours.

Charles L. Webster, and Clinton Bates, the latter a native of Chesterfield, were also members of Co. K, 52d regiment. They had not long resided in Easthampton, and of them we cannot speak particularly from personal acquaintance. They were, however, we think, held to be faithful and true to the service in which they had enlisted. Their lives were spared until the work of their regiment was nearly done, and they had looked forward to a reunion with their friends at home, in a short time. But God, who seeth not as man seeth, had another purpose, and they too were called away, and their bodies laid to rest beside the river which they had assisted to rescue from the hands of traitors.

The others, whose sacrifice and death remains to be chronicled, met their fate under circumstances more aggravating than did any of those before mentioned. We refer, of course, to those of our soldiers, who died in prison at Andersonville. Their names were, Alvin W.

Clark, Frederick P. Stone, Oliver A. Clark, Ezra O. Spooner, Rufus Robinson. All were members of Co. A, 27th regiment. The first two were original members of the company, and had been with it during most or all of its service. The next two went out as recruits in the summer of 1862, while the last entered upon the service in the early part of 1864. To all these, our deepest gratitude is due, not only for the service they performed, but for the extreme suffering they endured. For long, weary weeks or months, hungry and almost shelterless, in loneliness and sickness, with no tidings from home to cheer them up, no messages of love to light up the gloom. One after another, either from sickness without care, or from unsatisfied hunger, they passed away. They died with no kindly ministration, save the sympathy which their fellow prisoners could afford ; died with no hand of mother or sister to alleviate their pain, or to wipe the death damp from their brow ; died, perhaps, with no one near to whom they could tell their last messages of love and affection. Thus they died, and ever, among the greatest sacrifices for country, will be recorded that of those who perished at Andersonville.

Without any disparagement to the others, with whom we were less acquainted, we would say a word respecting Oliver A. Clark.

In early youth he was led to embrace the offers of salvation, became connected with the church, and always maintained a consistent Christian walk and conversation. But those whose privilege it has been to read his letters, and, especially since his death, to peruse his diary, cannot fail to have seen that the influence of his army life was to develop a deeper Christian experience and a firmer trust in God. While at home he was much engaged in the Sabbath school, of which at the time of his enlistment he was a director. During the winter of 1863-64, while stationed at Norfolk, he was employed as teacher or superintendent of a colored Sabbath school in that place, in which he took great interest. His friends at home were dear to him, but he felt that without a country to protect these, they could not be enjoyed, and he was willing to do what he could to defend that country whose interests he held so dear. In about three weeks after his arrival at the prison he was taken sick, and on the 27th of June he was removed from the stockade to the hospital. No one who knew him saw him after this. One of his companions, who attended upon him while he remained in the stockade, wrote in his diary, which has since been received by his friends, as follows: "He was perfectly resigned to whatever God's will might be, and such patience and faith did he exhibit, that we cannot but be sure that his was the peace which passeth understanding."

Charles Rensselear, a member of the 54th Mass. regiment, and a native of this town, was wounded in some battle, fell into the hands of the enemy, and was taken to Andersonville, where he died.

It has been said that the graves of her heroes are a nation's shrines, and as we have gathered, as it were, around the graves of these our heroes, surely it behooves us to tread lightly, for the place is sacred ground. Their forms we cannot see, for beneath the soil on which we stand they are mouldering to decay; but the spirit which actuated them still lives, and the principles for whose maintenance they died, though, indeed, triumphant to-day, will yet call for a vigorous defence. Here, while contemplating their character and death, surrounded as it were by their graves, may we be baptized anew by their spirit, and rededicate ourselves to the great cause to which they gave themselves.

The experiences of these four years of war, to those who remained at home, were wholly new and untried. They were such, moreover, as it is our sincere hope may never need to be repeated. Partings of friends we had seen before, but such partings as were in store for us, we knew not until war broke upon us. To look upon the manly form of one we loved, and to think that perhaps—ah! how the terrible possibilities come crowding in upon us—that, perhaps, he who was soon to go forth would never return; that, languishing in some hospital, or lying wounded and bleeding upon some field of carnage, death might come to him, this added to the separation a pang which words cannot tell. And when, amid gathering tears, the last words were said, and they gone from our homes, how we strained our eyes to catch a last glimpse of the loved ones. Eagerly we watched every mail that might bring to us letters from our soldiers in the field, and if a battle had occurred in which their regiment was likely to be engaged, how anxiously we looked over the published list of killed. No one can tell, unless he has experienced it, the sudden, crushing weight of sorrow, which falls on *their* hearts, who read there the name of the one dearest to them all. And then the anxiety for one who is in the hospital, wasting away with disease, the unrelieved anxiety which oppresses the hearts of those whose friends have been taken prisoners, and they can neither alleyiate their cruel sufferings nor hear of their fate, the eagerness with which the last weeks and days of their term of service are counted, and the anguish of those who look in vain, among the returning veterans, for the soldier who went forth from their homes, each of these feelings has been experienced by some in our midst; and, though the events are now passed, memory often renews them, and to the close of life, it will never cease to revert to those days of anxiety and sorrow.

Through the good Providence of God, a large proportion of those who enlisted have been spared to return home, and to enjoy the fruits of their hard earned victories.

In those homes where the vacant chair has not been, nor will be filled, we pray God to bestow his consolation, which may be more to them than the greatest earthly blessing.

To all who have manfully striven to uphold the government, our heartfelt gratitude is due, while those who return not, yet speak to us, bidding us take their places in the great struggle against wrong, and calling us to be true to ourselves, our country, and our God.

To God, the Almighty Disposer of Events, above all, should we render the highest tribute of gratitude and thanksgiving, for that he has upheld and defended us as a nation, and, at last, has brought about a return of peace.

Finally, by all which he has thus far done for us, and enabled us to do, in defending the constitution, and maintaining the principles of civil equality and religious freedom, let us entreat him to grant wisdom to those entrusted with the solution of the great problem of reconstruction, so that none of the fruits of victory, so dearly bought, may be lost, but that the grand work, so auspiciously begun by our valiant armies may be carried forward to a glorious consummation.

CHAPTER X.

GENEALOGICAL REGISTER.

GENEALOGY OF THE CLAPP FAMILY.

Capt. Roger Clapp was born in Salcom, Devonshire, England, the 6th day of April, 1609, of pious and creditable parents. His religious education was accompanied with the early strivings of the Holy Spirit, that ended in his conversion. In his younger years, he obtained leave of his father to live in the city of Exon, under the ministry of Rev. John Warham, to whom he was very much attached. In 1624, when Mr. Warham and Mr. Maverick (who were afterwards colleague pastors in Dorchester,) were preparing, with a considerable number of persons, to move to this country, Mr. Clapp found in himself a strong inclination to accompany them, and after having, with some difficulty, obtained leave of his father, he set himself to work, to assist in the great work which the people of God had then in hand. He left, as a legacy to his children, some account of God's remarkable Providences to him in bringing him to this land, and placing him here among his dear servants. The following is the account which he gives of his removal to this country, in his own words: "I gave you a hint towards the beginning that I came out of Plymouth, in Devon, the 20th of March, 1630; at Nantasket, (now Hull,) the 30th day of May,

1630. Now this is further to inform you that there came many goodly families in that ship. We were, of passengers, many in number, (besides seamen,) of good rank. Two of our magistrates came with us, viz., Mr. Rossiter and Mr. Ludlow. These godly people resolved to live together; and therefore, as they had made choice of those two Reverend servants of God, Mr. John Warham and Mr. John Maverick to be their ministers, so they kept a solemn day of fasting, in the new hospital in Plymouth, in England, spending it in preaching and praying; where that worthy man of God, Mr. John White of Dorchester, in Dorset, was present, and preached unto us the word of God, in the fore part of the day; and in the after part of the day, as the people did solemnly make choice of, and call those two godly ministers to be their officers, so also the Rev. Mr. Warham and Mr. Maverick, did accept thereof, and expressed the same. So we came, by the good hand of the Lord, through the deeps comfortably; having preaching or expounding of the word of God every day for ten weeks together, by our ministers. When we came to Nantasket, Capt. Squeb, who was captain of that great ship of four hundred tons, would not bring us into Charles river, as he was bound to do; but put us ashore, and our goods at Nantasket Point, and left us to shift for ourselves in a forlorn place in the wilderness. But as it pleased God, we got a boat of some old planters, and laded her with goods; and some able men, well armed, went in her unto Charlestown, where we found some wigwams and one house, and in that house there was a man, which had a boiled bass, but no bread that we saw, but we did eat of his bass, and then went up Charles river, until the river grew narrow and shallow, and there we landed our goods with much labor and toil, the bank being steep. And, night coming on, we were informed that there were, hard by us, three hundred Indians. One Englishman, that could speak the English language, an old planter, went to them and advised them not to come near us in the night; and they harkened to his counsel. I myself was one of the sentinels that night. Our captain was a low-country soldier, one Mr. Southcot, a brave soldier. In the morning some of the Indians came and stood at a distance off, looking at us, but came not near us; but when they had been awhile in view, some of them came and held out a great bass towards us; so we sent a man with a biscuit and changed the cake for the bass. Afterwards they supplied us with bass, exchanging a bass for a biscuit cake, and were very friendly unto us. Oh! Dear children! Forget not what care God had over his dear servants, to watch over us, and protect us in our weak beginnings. Capt. Squeb turned ashore us and our goods, like a merciless man, but God, even our merciful God, took pity on us, so that we were supplied, first with a boat, and then caused many Indians, (some hundreds,) to be rnled by the advice of one man not to come near us. Alas! had they come upon us, how soon might they have destroyed us! I think we were not above ten in number. But God caused the Indians to help us with fish at very cheap rates. We had not been there many days, (although by our diligence we had got up a kind of shelter, to save our goods in,) but we had orders to come away from that place, (which was about Watertown,) unto a place called Mattapan, now Dorchester, because there was a neck of land fit to keep our cattle on. So we removed and came to Mattapan. The Indians there, also, were kind unto us."

This was the first company that settled this side of Salem, and they met with many trials and difficulties, but Mr. Clapp was not at all disheartened, for his heart was taken off from temporal things, and seeing here such advantages for serving and glorifying God, he was led to exclaim, "Blessed be God that brought me here." In the same year that he came over here, he joined himself a member of the church in Dorchester, where he lived, and continued a member of this church for sixty years.

In 1633, in the twenty-fifth year of his age, he married Miss Joanna Ford, daughter of Mr. Thomas Ford, of Dorchester, in England, when she was but in the seventeenth year of her age. She, with her parents, came over in the same ship with himself, and settled also here in Dorchester. They lived together fifty-seven years. She was a godly and exemplary woman given to hospitality; she abounded in works of charity, so that, when proper objects of pity and charity came to her knowledge, she never failed to relieve them herself, or procure them relief from others. Thus the blessings of those that were ready to perish came upon her.

Mr. Clapp sustained both civil and military offices in the town, being captain of the militia, representative for the town, and authorized to join persons in marriage. On the 10th of August, 1665, the General Court appointed him captain of the Castle, (the principal fortress in the province,) which trust he discharged with great fidelity, and was therein serviceable to the whole province, and universally respected and honored. He continued in that place for twenty-one years, when he voluntarily resigned his command. An instance showing what an interest Capt. Clapp had in the hearts of God's people, and what an extensive blessing they accounted him is this:—

In the year 1672, he being the captain of the Castle, it pleased God to visit him with a fit of sickness; and the good people of Dorchester, unto which church he belonged, kept a day of fasting and prayer, to beg his life of God.

And God was pleased to hear and answer their prayers; and when he was restored to health, they kept a day of thanksgiving. When he left the Castle, in 1786, he removed to the south end of Boston, where he lived four years, and died February 2, 1791, in the eighty-second year of his age. His wife, who was born June 8, 1617, lived his widow between four and five years, and died at Boston, in June, 1095.

They had fourteen children, five of whom died in infancy, and three others, Thomas, who died at the age of fifteen years, Unite, at the age of seven, Supply, who was killed by the accidental firing of a gun in the Castle, at the age of twenty-three, were never married. The remaining six, four sons and two daughters, all had families. They were as follows:—Samuel, Elizabeth, Preserved, Hopestill, Wait, Desire. The daughters, Elizabeth and Wait, both lived in Boston.

Preserved, born Nov. 23, 1643, married Sarah Newberry of Windsor, and settled in Northampton. He was a useful citizen, and a great blessing to the town. He was a captain of the town, and their representative in the General Court, and ruling elder in the church. For a long time an Indian resided in his family, but he at length became unsteady, and wanted to get his gun, in which, however, he did not succeed. He finally left, and was gone for several years, when one day, as Mr. Clapp was riding home from his work, an Indian stepped out from behind a tree, and pointing his gun at him, said, "Now, 'Served, me have your gun," and instantly fired. The ball just grazed his nose. The Indian then stepped back again, but his leg was not concealed, so that the ball which was returned wounded him. Mr. Clapp then drove on as fast as possible, and eluded his pursuers, a company of Indians who had come from Canada with this one. The wound was so severe that it resulted in his death, and the party left for parts unknown.

Preserved Clapp had seven children who arrived at years of maturity, one of whom, Roger, was the father of Major Jonathan, one of the first settlers of Easthampton; of Aaron, who also settled in Easthampton; and of Roger, who lived in Southampton.

Major Jonathan Clapp came to Easthampton not far from 1730, and settled where Ansel Bartlett now resides. He was a man of keen foresight and great energy, and was very prominent in the early history of the town. He was the ancestor of nearly all the families in town who bear the name of Clapp. He had three sons and eight daughters, all of whom married, and lived to be over sixty years of age. They were Submit, who married Asahel Clark; Hannah, married Elias Lyman, who kept tavern in South Farms, Northampton, in the "old long house," which was recently torn down; Lois, married Jonathan Lyman; Beulah, married Rev. Solomon Allen, the first minister of Brighton, near Rochester, N. Y., from whom was descended Phineas Allen, late of Pittsfield, who for nearly sixty years was editor of the Pittsfield Sun; Rhoda married Col. Daniel Whittemore of Sunderland; Merab married Elisha Allen of Pittsfield; Lucy married Samuel Kellogg of Williamstown; Phebe married Joseph White of Springfield.

Jonathan Clapp, son of Major Jonathan, settled on the opposite side of the road, near his father, in the north part of the town. He was one of those mentioned in the notice of public houses. His children were five in number: Jonathan, Daniel, Medad, Mary, who married Ichabod Wright, and Margaret, who married Roswell Knight and afterwards John Ludden. Medad married Betsey Stebbins, and lived upon his father's place. He had two children,

Jonathan, who died young, and Lafayette, who is engaged in business in Easthampton.

Capt. Joseph Clapp, son of Maj. Jonathan, was a prominent citizen of the town. It was at his house that the church was organized, and in which, also, was held the meeting for the choice of officers, consequent upon the incorporation of the town of Easthampton. This house still stands, is now owned by Lucas W. Hannum, and formerly owned and occupied by Dea. Thaddeus Clapp. The sons of Capt. Joseph were Joseph, Thaddeus, Rufus, Isaac and Luther. He had, besides, two daughters, one of whom died in early life, and the other, Elizabeth, married Eliakim Phelps of Chesterfield, who afterwards settled in Northampton. She lived to be over eighty years of age.

Joseph was a merchant for a number of years. He was for a time one of the most influential men in the place. He filled the office of town clerk for a longer period than any other man, with one exception. In 1810 he retired from mercantile life, but remained here until 1830, when he removed to Homer, N. Y., with his son Joseph. He had ten children, of whom two, Sumner G. and Aleander, were graduates of Yale College. The former was ordained and settled in the gospel ministry at Enfield, afterwards at Cabotville, St. Johnsbury, Vt., and Sturbridge. The latter studied theology at Andover, and was licensed to preach. He taught school in one of the Southern States, and afterwards at Worthington and Pittsfield. Alonzo, another son, engaged in mercantile pursuits in Illinois.

Dea. Thaddeus was born March 31, 1770. He kept tavern for many years, and also, in connection with his father, owned and worked a fulling mill. In 1808 he was chosen deacon of the church, which office he held for thirty-three years, and during this time, as well as after his resignation of the office, until his death, was a faithful supporter of the institutions of religion. In civil affairs he was no less prominent. He was the first justice of the peace appointed in the town, and was its treasurer for twenty years. While Easthampton was a district, it was only represented in the General Court, by the privilege of voting in connection with Northampton. The united population of the two places were entitled to three representatives. On one occasion, when considerable interest was felt in the election, and perhaps some doubt as to the result, the Federalists of Northampton sent out word that if Easthampton would unite upon a man, they would support him. Dea. Clapp was the man selected as candidate. He was elected, and represented the town in the General Court for twelve years, before the close of which time the district had been incorporated as a town. He was delegate to the convention held in Northampton in 1812, to consider the duty of government on the war question, and also delegate to the constitutional convention of the State.

He had seven children who arrived at years of maturity. Mary married Justus Merrill of Pittsfield, where she now resides; Elvira married Ansel Bartlett; Philena married Spencer Clark; Thaddeus moved to Pittsfield, where he engaged in manufacturing. Theodore graduated at Yale college in 1814, studied theology, was ordained and settled as pastor of the First Congregational church in New Orleans. Thornton W. graduated at Williams College in 1830, was professor of mathematics in Washington college, Miss., studied theology, and was licensed to preach the gospel in the Episcopal church, and preached some years. Luther has been employed in business in his native place, where he now resides.

Isaac, brother of Dea. Thaddeus, settled in the center of the town, a few rods south of where the Payson church now stands. For many years he was joint partner of the flouring mill in the place, in addition to which he carried on a farm. He had five children:—Marilla, who married Edwin Kingsley of Southampton; Judith, who married Theodore Lyman; Isaac K., who married Alice, daughter of Sylvester Knight, and now resides in Easthampton; Maria Ann and Edward, who also live in their native town.

Luther, the youngest son of Capt. Joseph, married Tirzah, daughter of Dea. Enoch White of South Hadley. He kept tavern quite a number of years previous to his death, which occurred in 1811. His wife, who died about the same time, was buried in the same grave, and a monument erected over it which bears the following inscription:— "In memory of Capt. Luther Clapp, who died Aug. 17, aged 39 years, and his wife, Mrs. Tirzah Clapp, who died the 31st, same month, A. D. 1811, aged 38 years. Both fell victims to the typhoid fever. They were active, pleasing, benevolent, devout.

For us no longer mourn,
Your souls demand your care,
Soon you'll be hither borne,
For death, O friends, prepare.

Insatiate archer! could not one suffice? Thy shaft flew twice, and twice it smote full sore. Scarce did the widowed mourner from the cold grave of a loved partner trace her backward steps, than death his awful mandate sent to call her home. Two weeks she struggled with disease, when death released her from her sufferings here, to soar on angel wings to realms of bliss. This once happy pair, who here repose, no children left their early exit to lament, but many friends who their sad fate will long bemoan. Rich in the comforts of domestic bliss, blest with the ample gifts of fortune, and more blessed with ample hearts, disposed to sweetest acts of charity."

Quartermaster Benjamin Clapp, youngest son of Major Jonathan, was born in 1728, married Phebe Boynton from Coventry, Ct., and settled on the plain south of the center of the town. He was a soldier in the Revolutionary war for some time, but was obliged to leave the army to take charge of his father, who was taken sick in the army just before the battle of Bennington, and at the time of the action was in Pittsfield, and could hear distinctly the cannon roar, which so fired his youthful patriotism that he longed to participate in the engagement, and expressed this desire to his father, who replied, "No, my son, you must stay and take care of me." He died in 1815, at the age of seventy-seven. At the time of his death his mental faculties were very much impaired, and had been for some years. On the subject of religion, however, his mind continued bright till the last. Prayer and communion with his Saviour were his delightful employments. His wife survived him thirty-two years, and died in December, 1847, at the advanced age of ninety-seven years. She had a very genial disposition, and retained her activity, both of body and mind, till the last year of her life.

They had five sons and eight daughters, who arrived at years of maturity. Two children died in infancy. Rachel, born February 28, 1768, married Nathaniel Edwards of Northampton, where she still resides, at the advanced age of ninety-eight. Sophia married Rev. Gad Newell of Nelson, N. H., whose daughter is the wife of Rev. John S. Emerson, missionary to the Sandwich Islands. Anna married Medad Lyman of Northampton, who afterwards moved to Charlotte, Vt.; Clarissa married Jonathan Lyman; Sally married Daniel Lyman; Phebe married Levi Clapp; Fanny married Jared Clark; Caroline married Milton Knight, who lives now in Westhampton.

The sons were Ocran, Solomon, Spencer, Benjamin and George. The first three settled in Easthampton. Ocran married Mrs. Sarah Brown, daughter of Captain David Lyman. His sons, Lorenzo and Algernon, moved to the West. His daughters were Florilla, Climena and Lucy, the last of whom married Milton Lloyd of Blandford, whose son, I. Homer, is now a resident of this place. Solomon lived on the place occupied by his father. He married Paulina Avery. Their children were ten in number. William N. resides in Easthampton; Emelus, Benjamin, Solomon and Theodore removed to Ohio; George is a farmer in Minnesota; Mariette is the wife of Joseph F. Alvord; Sophia married Lavater Lewis of Westfield; Jane E., wife of Z. A. Thayer; Amelia, wife of Wm. Hart of Lebanon, Ohio. Spencer, son of Benjamin, Sen., born 1784, lived in the house built by Sergeant Corse, who first cleared the road leading from his house north to the center of the town, a distance of more than a mile in a direct line. The children of Spencer are, Alfred, who lives in Huntington; Nelson, who lives in Plainfield; Spencer, with whom his father now lives, in Winsted, Ct.; Eliza, who died in early life; Caroline, wife of Jared Smith of Granby; and Lewis, who resides in Easthampton.

Aaron Clapp, brother of Major Jonathan, was among the first settlers on the plain. His wife was Jemima Bartlett. Their children were Ensign, Aaron, who removed to western New York in 1808; David, who was a soldier in the Revolutionary war, and never returned; Jemima; Achsah; Eli, who removed to Southampton; Levi, who was a Revolutionary soldier, and afterwards settled in Easthampton. He had only two children who lived to mature years: Levi, who inherited his estate, and Jerusha, who married William Perkins of Southampton. Levi married Phebe Clapp. Their children were: Austin, who died young; Lucius, who lived with his father; and Achsah, wife of James H. Lyman.

John Clapp, a nephew of Major Jonathan and Aaron, was also a soldier of the Revolution. He settled in the west part of the town, where his son John afterwards lived. The children of John Jr. are: Sophia, wife of Sylvester Cooper; Maurice, John M., Amos B., all of whom live in their native town; Asa D. and Eliakim, who have moved away.

Another son of John Clapp, Sen., was James, who lived in the center of the town. His children were Adaline, Helen and James, the former of whom is the wife of Robert Dewar. James resides in Worcester.

GENEALOGY OF THE CLARK FAMILY.

"The name Clark was derived from the name of an office, and signified clerk, or learned man. This title, in process of time, became the surname of the person who held the office, and 'Clericus,' afterwards Clark, became the cognomen or surname by which all his descendants were distinguished. The word 'clerk' was also abundantly employed in the north of England, to express lawyer as well as priest, and this accounts for the extreme frequency of the name." In an ancient record of Surrey, in the county of Durham, England, among many others, we find the following entry: "Gulielmus Clercus tenet triginta acras et reddit unam marcam."—"William Clark holds 30 acres, for which he pays one mark." A mark was 13s. 4d.

The first person of this name, who came to this country, was Lieut. William Clark, who was born in England, probably in Plymouth, in Devonshire, in 1609. He was in Dorchester as early as 1638. From there he came to Northampton, probably in 1659. He was chosen one of the town's-men or select-men, in March, 1660, and representative to the "Great and General Court" in 1663. He was one of the eight members of the church in Northampton at its organization, June 18, 1661. He died July 12, 1690, aged 81. His wife Sarah, died Sept. 6, 1675. He was selectman nineteen years, and bore the title of "the Most Worshipful William Clark." For a long time he was one of the commissioners, or judges, of the county courts.

He had nine children, one of whom, Samuel by name, had a son Samuel, whose son, Benjamin, was the father of Phineas Clark, who settled in the east part of the town, on a farm now owned by Bryant Pendleton. Several of his brothers and sisters were among the early inhabitants of Westhampton, one of whom, Elizabeth, was the mother of Rev. Justin Edwards, D. D., the well known divine, at one time President of Andover Theological Seminary. During the Revolutionary War, Mr. Clark served three years in the army. An incident is told of him which is interesting. On one occasion, while on guard, he discovered a man in the garb of an officer, approaching him. He hailed him with the customary, "Who's there." "A friend," was the reply." "Give the countersign," said he. "I can't do it, but my business is very urgent, I must pass." "Not without the countersign." "I am entrusted with business of great importance." The officer had by this time advanced almost within reach of his bayonet. "Advance another step," said the guard, "and I'll run you through with my bayonet." The whole tone and manner of the officer changed. "I guess you are a good soldier. I can trust you." It was General Washington.

Again, after a tiresome march, he was placed on guard, and being young and in poor health, he fell asleep. In this condition he was found by a soldier, and reported to the commanding officer. He was tried, and sentenced to one day's imprisonment in the guard-house. His punishment would have been death, had it not been for the voluntary and earnest efforts of his comrades from Northampton, who plead that his state of health was such that he *ought* to have been, and *had before* been, excused from guard duty. The event proved to him a great blessing. The next day was exceedingly hot, and some of his comrades died from the exertions which they were compelled to make. Such would probably have been his fate, but for the confinement.

In 1787, he was taken prisoner by the Shay's insurrectionists, in consequence of the loyalty of his sentiments, though from his state of health he had had no part in the endeavors to suppress rebellion. He was released, however, on the third day, much to the relief of his family, who knew not what had befallen him, since he was taken while absent from home. His wife was Elizabeth White of Hadley, who outlived him thirty-eight years, and died in 1847, after being permitted to see more than seventy of their descendants. Their children were as follows: —Submit, who was the wife of Jonathan Parsons of South Farms, Northampton; Elihu, who now resides in Granville; Sylvester, who settled in the practice of medicine in Boston, Erie county, N. Y.; Salome, wife of Rufus Smith, formerly of South Hadley and Worthington, but now of Huntington; Lucinda, who was the wife of Justin Cook of Northampton; Silence, wife of Asa Marble of Worthington; Elizabeth, wife of Elisha King of Westhampton; Erastus, settled in West Farms, Northampton; Paulina lives in Westhampton; Lydia, wife of Medad King of Westhampton; Amanda, wife of Maurice Parsons, of Worthington; Persis died in childhood.

Dea. John Clark, son of William Clark of Northampton, had twelve children. It is of him that the late President Dwight, in his "Travels in New England and New York," says: "One specimen of longevity and multiplication, in a single family, deserves to be recorded. Dea. John Clark, son of William Clark, Esq., had twelve children. One died in infancy. Six sons and five daughters had families. Ebenezer, the third son, died February 27, 1781, aged 98 years. Josiah, the youngest son, died April 7, 1789, aged 81. From the six sons, were descended 1158 children, grand-children, and great-grandchildren, 928 of whom were living at the time of Josiah's death."

The oldest of these sons, Dea. John Clark, Jr., was born Dec. 28, 1679, and married Elizabeth Cook of Hartford, great-grand-daughter of Major Aaron Cook. He had eleven children, from two of whom, Eliakim and Ithamar, have descended a large majority of the persons in town, who bear this name. A daughter, Catharine, married Dea. Samuel Edwards of Southampton, who was the grandfather of Rev. Bela B. Edwards.

Eliakim removed to Easthampton, and settled in Pascommuck. It was he who gave the land for the burial-place now used in that part of the town. He had three sons and eight daughters. All the sons, Obadiah, Asahel, and Job, settled near their father.

Three of the daughters married in Easthampton. Esther married Jonathan Janes, Lydia married Lemuel Lyman, Huldah married Nathaniel White.

Of the sons before mentioned, Lieut. Asahel was born Feb. 17, 1737, and married Submit Clapp. He was in the battle of Lake George, Sept. 8, 1755. He did not belong to the scouting party commanded by Col. Williams, but with others was left in defence of the fort from which this party set out. He bravely aided in the repulse of the enemy under Baron Dieskeau, as they rushed on, greatly elated with their success in the defeat of the scouting party. Lieut. Clark was also at Ticonderoga, three years after, when the British were defeated, with great carnage, in their attempt to take the fortress. British pride, on that occasion, saved the colonial troops from slaughter, since they were not allowed to participate in the assault. In 1788, a call was issued for volunteers to defend the arsenal at Springfield, against the attack of the Shay's party. The people of the town had responded to the call; a company under the command of Capt. David Lyman, were already at Springfield. News however came that more men were wanted, and another company was formed, consisting of about forty men from South and Easthampton, most of them either older or younger than the members of the first. They had marched as far as the house of Elias Lyman, in the south part of Northampton, when, to their surprise, they discovered a party of 400 men, whom they knew by the badge which they wore —a sprig of evergreen in their hats—to be Shay's men. There was not the slightest hope of successful resistance against such overwhelming odds, and they were taken prisoners. Lieut. Clark, then fifty years of age, was a member of this company. He was a man of high spirit, and could not well brook the thought of falling into the hands of a set of men, whom he despised from his inmost soul. Hoping to escape observation, he stepped into the house of Mr. Lyman near by, neglecting, however, to remove the slip of white paper which the loyalists wore in their hats as a badge. The troops passed on, but, unfortunately, for him, one of the insurgents came in, and, seeing by the badge that he was a loyalist, seized him and drove him along with his gun. Before they had proceeded very far, Mr. Clark who had no gun, watching his opportunity, sprang upon his captor and attempted to disarm him, in which attempt however, he was unsuccessful. His resistance so exasperated the ruffian, that, despite his age, he dealt him a heavy blow upon his head, wounding him severely. This band of insurgents, which was from Berkshire County, marched to Pelham, where they retained their prisoners for about one week, when they were permitted to return. Lieut. Clark afterwards recovered damage from the person who took him prisoner. He died Feb. 17, 1822, on his 85th birthday. He had twelve children. His sons, Eliakim, Eleazer, Asahel, and Bohan, settled in Easthampton, and reared up families. Eliakim, however, afterwards removed to Otisco, N. Y., where he died.

Horace L., son of Anson Clark, of West Springfield, and grandson of Eliakim, with the exception of a son of Asahel, who bears up his name, is the only descendant of this branch of the family who lives in the place.

Jared, another son of Lieut. Asahel, married Fanny Clapp and removed to Brecksville, Ohio. Charles removed to Otisco, N. Y., where he still resides. Two sons died in early life. Submit, the oldest daughter, married Ebenezer Janes, Electa was the wife of Elam Rumrill, Jerusha wife of Caleb Loud of Loudville, Achsah wife of Daniel Wright, formerly of Easthampton, but afterwards of Huntsburg, Ohio.

Obadiah Clark, son of Eliakim, Sen., settled where his grandson Zenas now resides. He was a man of unusual attainments in piety and spirituality.

His family consisted of six children, Zenas and Gaius who died young; Esther, who died at the age of thirty-one; Jemima, who married Stephen Wood, Clarrissa, who married Andrew Howard of West Springfield; Thaddeus, who married Tamasind, daughter of Ezekiel Wood, and settled in his native place. He was an earnest Christian and a pillar in the church to which he belonged. He had six children, of whom one died in infancy and two others, Thaddeus and Philena, died unmarried, though they lived to mature years. The other three, Obadiah, Zenas, and Deacon E. Alonzo, are now residents of the town.

Job Clark, son of Eliakim, Sen., and brother of Lieut Asahel, was born Sept. 10, 1733, and married Eunice Strong. He built the house where his grandson, Henry Clark now resides. He had six children. Sereno and Ruth died in early life; Eunice married Asa Ferry; Luther moved to Skaneateles, N. Y., but afterwards returned; Spencer settled in Easthampton; Job, who graduated at Williams College, studied medicine, and practised many years in Westfield. He now resides in Massilon, Ohio.

Luther married Deborah Robinson, and lived on his father's place. He had five sons, all of whom settled in Easthampton, viz.: Luther, Alanson, Jason, Horace, Henry. The four last named are at present resident in town. The oldest, Capt. Luther Clark, died in 1865. He had been a man of considerable influence in town, had several times represented it in the Legislature, and had, during a period of eighteen years, served on the board of selectmen. In this family there was also five daughters, Emeline, wife of Ozro C. Wright of Northampton, Maria, wife of Luther M. Fairfield of Holyoke, Harriet, who died in early life, Elvira, Cordelia, wife of Theodore Clark.

Ithamar Clark, son of Dea. John, Jr., and brother of Eliakim, Sen., was a resident of Northampton. His family consisted of nine sons and one daughter. One of the sons, Oliver, born Jan. 13, 1756, moved to Easthampton, and built a house in the west part of the town, where the widow of Dea. Ithamar Clark until recently, resided. He was married twice, and was the father of nineteen children. Of these, Azariah, born Sept. 17, 1778, graduated at Williams College in 1805, being the first inhabitant of Easthampton who received a collegiate education. He studied theology; was settled in Canaan, N. Y.; afterwards removed to Colebrook, Ct., where he died in 1832. Julius, born Dec. 17, 1779, had a family of seven children, lived in Northampton, on the place now occupied by Abner Wade. Simeon, the oldest son, was born Feb. 10, 1777, and spent the greater part of his life in Easthampton. He was a carpenter by trade, and was often entrusted with the care of difficult pieces of work. Among other things, he built a bridge across Mill river in Northampton, about the year 1820. He finally went to Huntsburg, Ohio, where he died. His children were eight in number, viz: Simeon Parsons, Coleman, Mercy, Tertius, Esther, Lewis, Diana, Abner Laurens. The oldest, Simeon Parsons, lived in his native town, and followed the occupation of his father. He was the father of Edmund W. and George P. Clark, the former of whom now resides here. Coleman and Lewis now live in Ohio; Mercy married Abner Wade; Tertius, recently deceased, occupied the old place; Laurens is at present an inhabitant of the town, though he has most of the time lived elsewhere.

Another son of Oliver Clark, Sen., was Oliver, who was born August 17, 1785. He settled on a part of the old homestead of his father. He was a very active, energetic man. In 1820 he was chosen Captain of the Militia Company and was engaged to some extent in public business. He died at the early age of thirty-seven, leaving six sons, viz: Rufus, Josephus, Lysander, Nelson, Frederick, and John Milton, the last of whom owns and carries on the farm of his father. Lysander resides in Clyde, N. Y., Nelson in Easthampton, and Frederick in Springfield. Rufus moved to Hartford, Ct., and Josephus to Aurora, Ind., where they died.

Dea. Ithamar, the youngest son of Oliver Clark, Sen., was born October 27, 1802. He was killed April 3d, 1857, while engaged in drawing stone. He was the father of Rev. Edson L. Clark, who graduated at Yale College, studied theology at Union Theological Seminary, and is now pastor of the Congregational church in Dalton.

Capt. Philip Clark, a second cousin of Lieut. Asahel and of Oliver, was in the fourth generation from Lieut. William, who first came from England. He lived in Pascommuck, was one of the first school-teachers in the town, was also one of the forty-six original members of the church, and its first clerk. Although politically opposed to a majority of the voters, he was as prominent in town affairs as any one. He was quite frequently chosen to preside over the deliberations of the town, and for a number of years filled the position of selectman with credit. He has quite a numerous posterity.

Elam Clark, his son, married Dorcas Brown, and settled in Pascommuck. He had six daughters, four of whom married in Easthampton. Dorcas, wife of Parsons Janes ; Rachel, wife of Lyman Avery ; Triphenia, wife of John Wright ; and Dorothy, wife of Solomon Ferry. The oldest son, Elam C. Clark, graduated in Williams College in 1812, studied theology, and was ordained pastor of a church in Providence, R. I. He died in Suffield, Ct. Julius lived on the old homestead, where two of his sons, Julius F., and Austin P., now reside. His oldest son, Sheldon, also lives in the town. His daughter Celia married Joseph Parsons, Bela lived where his son, Theodore, now does. He had a family of five sons, viz : Theodore, William, Edward, Alfred, Charles.

Uriel Clark, another son of Capt. Philip, married Hannah Janes, Dec. 30, 1782, and settled on the old homestead. He had two daughters, one of whom, Susannah, married Manly Street, and the other, Anna, married Chauncey Parsons. He had also three sons, Uriel, Saul, and Philip. Philip inherited his father's estate. He had five children, Lawrence, Uriel, Gilbert A., Melancey, Martha, of whom the last mentioned was the first wife of J. Emerson Lyman. The sons Uriel and Gilbert A., now reside on their father's place, which, it will be seen, has descended, through successive generations, to its present owners.

GENEALOGY OF THE LYMAN FAMILY.

The coat of arms of the Lyman family may be thus described. Arms—azure, on which appear 3 dolphins, natant. Crest—a sword unsheathed. Underneath the shield, on a band, is inscribed the motto, "*Factis non Verbis*,"—"By deeds not words." In regard to the dolphin as an armorial bearing Sloane's Evan's British Heraldry says:—"The dolphin which is a much esteemed and ancient bearing has been said to be the hieroglyphic of Charity, Parental Affection and Society, there being no other fish which loves the society of men." The unsheathed sword would seem to refer to some military achievement of the ancestors, or perhaps to the readiness of the family to meet the calls of patriotism. The above described coat of arms is found in one branch of the Lyman family; but it would seem not to be universally accepted as the coat of arms of the family, since there is, in another branch, one differing somewhat from this, though having points of resemblance.

Richard Lyman came from England in 1631, in the time of King Charles I, and settled in Roxbury, where he lived in some state, having two servants. He was a member of the church of Rev. John Elliot. He brought with him his wife Sarah, and five children, Phillis, Richard, Sarah, John and Robert. Late in the year 1635, he removed through the woods with others to Hartford. On his way thither, he lost some of his cattle, and suffered much the ensuing winter at Hartford, in consequence of which he became melancholy, though he afterwards recovered from this state of mind. "He was an ancient Christian, but weak, yet, after some years of trial and quickening, he joined the church." His name, with ninety-nine others, first settlers of Hartford, is inscribed on a monument in an ancient cemetery in that place. He died in the year 1640.

His three sons, Richard, John and Robert, were among the first settlers in Northampton in 1655, and all died there, leaving families, though Robert had no male issue. He was a hunter and trapper, and is said to have perished on Roberts' Hill. He discovered the lead mines in the south-west part of Northampton, which are noticed in the ancient records of that town. Richard had a numerous posterity, some of whom settled in Lebanon, Ct. Another branch went to Durham, Ct., while another remained at Northampton.

Lieut. John Lyman, son of Richard, was born in England, in September, 1623, and died August 20, 1690. He was in command of the Northampton soldiers, in the famous Falls fight above Deerfield, May 18, 1676. His wife was Dorcas Plum of Branford, Ct. The American House, which was burnt a few years since in Northampton, stood in front of his house lot. His children were, Elizabeth, Sarah, John, Moses, Dorothy, Mary, Experience, Joseph, Benjamin, and Caleb. The oldest son, John, was born in 1661, married Mindwell Sheldon in 1687, and died November 8, 1740. In the latter part of his life, he lived east of Mt. Tom, and kept a public house, where his son Elias, afterwards kept tavern, near Smith's Ferry.

Benjamin, another of the sons, was born in 1674. He married Thankful, a grand-daughter of Eltweed Pomeroy, who came from England. Their family consisted of nine sons and three daughters, viz: Joseph, Benjamin, Benjamin, Aaron, Caleb, William, Daniel, Elihu, Medad, Eunice, Hannah, and Susannah. Joseph settled in Northampton, and was the father of Joseph and Elisha, the former of whom was the father of Judge Joseph Lyman, who graduated at Yale College in 1783, and grandfather of Samuel F. Lyman, Esq., now Judge of Probate and Insolvency. William was the father of Gen. William Lyman, who was at one time consul at London. Daniel removed to New Haven, and engaged in mercantile pursuits.

Benjamin was born in 1703, and married Mary Mosely of Glastenbury, Ct. He, together with Stephen Wright, purchased "School Meadow," and afterwards moved to Easthampton, and built a house where Joel Bassett now resides. He was one of the early and constant supporters of Rev. Jonathan Edwards. He was one of the nineteen who voted to retain him as pastor of the church in Northampton, at the time of the opposition to him. He died in 1762, aged 59. His children were Benjamin, born in 1727; Lemuel, born in 1735; David, born in 1737; and four daughters, Molly, Thankful, Esther and Patty Capt. David lived where S. M. Lyman now does. He has no descendants of the Lyman name. He had four daughters who married and lived in this town. They were as follows: Sarah, who first married Eli Brown and afterwards Ocran Clapp; Eunice married Job Strong, the father of A. L. Strong; Rachel married Sylvester Knight, who was the father of Hon. H. G. Knight; Fidelia was the wife of Solomon Pomeroy.

Benjamin built a house on the plain, where his grandson, Rev. Solomon Lyman, now lives. He was very active and influential in the formation of the church and district. To him was directed the warrant, to call together the citizens to the first meeting of the district after its organization. Robert Breck, Esq., who was empowered by act of General Court to issue his warrant to some prominent citizen, was chosen Moderator of the first meeting. Mr. Lyman was chosen Moderator of the second meeting, and he occupied that position many times thereafter. In church matters, he was also a leader. Before the settlement of a pastor, it was needful that there be a moderator, who could legally call meetings of the church, an office to which he was appointed. At one of the earliest business meetings of the church, he was chosen Deacon, which office he accepted, and performed its duties till his death in June, 1798. He was a man of ardent piety, a faithful servant of Christ, and when he laid his armor down, we doubt not, he entered upon his reward.

His children were Benjamin, Solomon, Hannah, Polly, Ruth, Dorotha, and Mercy. The daughters all married, removed from town, and all lived past middle life. Of the sons, the first mentioned built a house, where his grandson, Ansel B., now lives. Solomon remained on his father's place. He married Lois, daughter of Jonathan Janes, Sen. In 1807, he was chosen deacon, in which capacity he served eighteen years. His family consisted of four daughters and one son. The daughters were, Theodosia, Lois, Susan, and Mercy. His son Solomon graduated at Yale College in 1822, studied theology, was ordained a minister of the gospel, settled in Keesville, N. Y., afterwards at Poultney, Vt. He now resides in his native town.

The family of Benjamin were Jeremiah, Theodorus, who lives in Ohio, Polly, Eunice, Clarissa, Ansel, and Louisa, the last two of whom died in youth. The oldest occupied his father's place, and spent his life there. His family consisted of the following children, viz:—Theresa, who married Rev. Addison Lyman, and died in Geneseo, Ill.; Louisa, who married James O. Waite of Hatfield; Ansel B., who is a resident of this town; Adelle S., and Henry Martyn, who until recently has resided in Minnesota.

Lemuel Lyman, born August 28, 1735, married Lydia, daughter of Eliakim Clark, and lived on his father's place. He was in the memorable battle of Lake George, September 8, 1775. Soon after this, he, with others, was sent with a drove of cattle for the northern army. It was supposed, that, in this expedition, by the privations and exposures which he endured, he laid the foundation for the rheumatism, a disease, which in later years, rendered him to some extent, unable to perform manual labor. He was a member of the board of selectmen for seven years, and one of the leaders in the establishment of a church, and the erection of a house of worship. He was a man of great physical strength, and was quick to perceive the best method of action in a moment of danger. He had a very retentive memory, great presence of mind, and native energy of character. He died July 16, 1810, aged 74. His children were Lydia, who married Ebenezer K. Rust of Southampton, Lemuel, Justus, Ahira, Sylvester, Daniel, Esther, who married Obadiah Janes, and Elihu. All the sons settled in Easthampton, and were men of considerable influence in the town, and all have posterity residing here at the present day.

Capt. Lemuel, married Olive Lyman of Norwich. His trade was that of carpenter and joiner, although he owned and lived on a farm. About the year 1800, he superintended the removal of a dam across the Connecticut river at South Hadley Canal, which stood about two miles above the present dam, and set the water back into the meadows, occasioning much sickness. In answer to a petition on the subject the legislature ordered its removal. His children were Dwight, Theodore, Dennis, and Theodosia, all of whom lived in their native town. Theodosia married Augustus Clapp.

Justus owned and occupied a farm adjoining that of his brother. He was a man of influence in the affairs of the town, which he served in the capacity of selectman, eleven years. He had three children, George, Charles, and E. Waldo, the latter of whom settled on his father's place.

Ahira located himself on the plain, west of the center, building for himself the house now occupied by Elijah A. Lyman. He was a very active and prosperous business man, both as a farmer and mechanic. His death occurred November 1, 1836, in consequence of a severe wound in his foot, made by an axe. His children were, Roland, who removed to Lowell, where he now resides, Lemuel P., Ahira, Quartus P., William, and Jabez B., the latter of whom graduated at Amherst College in 1841, resided in Germany some years, where he was a student in one of the Universities. He was afterwards principal of a Female Seminary in Abbeville, S. C. He was for a time established as an oculist in Chicago, but for several years has been engaged in the practice of surgery in Rockford, Ill. The others mentioned remained in their native place, except Ahira, who lived on Park Hill, just within the limits of Northampton. He, however, now resides in Easthampton.

Sylvester lived on the place first purchased by Benjamin Lyman, on his removal from Northampton, owning and working the farm. He was chosen deacon in 1813, and continued in the office twenty years. His children were, S. Mosely, who lives in his native place, Ursula, who was the first wife of Dea. Ithamar Clark, Naomi, who married Warren. Montague of Sunderland, Sylvester, who resides in Hartford, J. Emerson, who died a few years since in his native place, Elizabeth, wife of E. L. Snow, Tirzah, wife of E. S. Hoadley, and Edwin who lives in Bridgeport, Ct.

Daniel married Sally, daughter of Benjamin Clapp, and lived on Park Hill, where his son, Lauren D., now lives. He was a man of more than ordinary religious feeling, a devoted friend and warm supporter of the institutions of religion, and a pillar in the prayer-meetings of the church and neighborhood. He died September 23, 1853. His children were Daniel F., Josiah, Addison, Horace, Sarah B., Lauren D., and James H. Josiah graduated at Williams College in 1836, studied Theology, was licensed to preach, afterwards principal of an academy in Williston, Vt., and then of the academy in Lenox, where he still lives. Addison graduated at Williams College in 1839, studied Theology, entered the service of the Home Missionary Society, and is now a preacher in Sheffield, Ill. He was for a time principal of an academy in Geneseo, Ill. Horace graduated at Williams College in 1842, ordained an evangelist, and was employed as a Home Missionary at Portland, and Dallas, Oregon. He is now Professor of Mathematics, in Pacific University, at Forest Grove in that state. He went to Oregon about the time of the California gold excitement, and was largely instrumental in the gathering of two churches at the places mentioned. The primary object of the institution in which he is now engaged is to raise up men to supply the need of ministerial labor there. The other sons, Daniel F., Lauren D., and James H., are citizens of their native town.

Elihu, the youngest and only surviving son, lives at present with his son William J. in this town. In early life he intended to get an education, and for this purpose entered Williams College, of which he was a member until the Junior year, when he was compelled to leave in consequence of weakness of eyes. He has lived since in New Lebanon, N. Y., and in Williamsburg, but spent the greater portion of the active period of life in his native town. His children were Alfred E., who settled in Williamsburg, but now resides in Brooklyn; Eliza, who married John G. Mallory; William J.; Mary Ann, who married William Leonard; Cornelia, who married Elisha H. Rice; Nancy, who was the wife of Thaddeus K. Wright of Westhampton. Three children, Martha, Ann Jane, and Curtis, died unmarried. William J. is the only one of these children who now reside in their native place. For many years he carried on the business of wagon making in this town, but for some years past has been employed as a patent right dealer, and also as a patentee.

GENEALOGY OF THE WRIGHT FAMILY.

Dea. Stephen Wright, one of the purchasers of School Meadow, was a great-grandson of Dea. Samuel Wright, one of the first settlers of Springfield. He was a resident of that town as early as 1641. After Rev. Mr. Moxon, first minister of Springfield, returned to England, Dea. Wright "was employed to dispense the word of God in this place," and was allowed fifty shillings a month for his services. Other laymen were also employed in the same way. Dea. Wright was also one of the first settlers of Northampton, whither he removed in 1656 or 7, and where he died in 1665. His brother, Nathaniel, was a merchant in London, and was interested in the Winthrop Colony in 1630. Their father, it is said, was John

Wright, of Kelvedon, and their grandfather, John Wright, of Wrightsbridge, in Essex, about forty miles east of London.

Samuel Wright, oldest son of Dea. Samuel, lived in Northampton. One of his sons, Capt. Benjamin, was a noted Indian fighter, and was finally slain by them at Northfield. Another son, Samuel, had eight children, one of whom, Stephen, was chosen deacon of the church in Northampton, in 1739, but removed to Easthampton, probably about 1744. His house, which stood where Samuel Hurlburt now lives, on the hill just west of Sawmill brook, then stood within the limits of Southampton. Sergeant Eliakim Wright, his son, was killed in the battle of Lake George. Job, another son, graduated at Yale College in 1757, and was settled in the ministry at Bernardston, where he died. In this connection it may not be uninteresting to remark, that when he graduated, and for several years thereafter, the names of the graduates were not arranged alphabetically, but according to the standing of the family to which they belonged.

Stephen, another of the sons, married Catherine Sheldon, daughter of Noah Sheldon, of Southampton. He settled on the plain south of the meeting house, and built the house until recently occupied by his grandson, John Wright. In 1786 he was chosen deacon of the church, in which capacity he served twenty-one years.

His children were Catherine, who died in childhood, Eliakim, Stephen, Catherine, who married Justin Clark of Southampton, Gideon, Noah, Hezekiah, Luther. Eliakim, born in 1757, married Mrs. Martha Matthews, widow of Dea. Gideon Matthews of Chester. He lived a little way north of his father's residence. He was a man of more than ordinary ability, and possessed of good judgment, though somewhat eccentric. In early life he entertained the idea of preparing for the ministry, but he finally abandoned it. His piety was of a deep and earnest type, and exercised a controlling influence over his life.

Stephen, born in 1758, married Sarah Lyman, daughter of Dea. John Lyman of Southampton, and settled in the south part of the town. His daughter, Sarah, married Zenas Clark, and Lucy married John Wright. His oldest son, John, succeeded to his estate. He was an energetic and prosperous farmer, and acquired considerable property. He died in December, 1857.

Hezekiah lived on the old homestead, where his son, John Wright, now lives. His daughter, Dorotha, married Luke Janes, Abigail married Sidney Ferry, Harriet married John Y. Smith, a resident of Madison, Wis. Besides these, there were three children, John the oldest, who died in infancy, Hezekiah, who died at the age of twenty-six, and Emily, who died in early life.

Luther married Sarah Lyman, daughter of Jonathan Lyman of Northampton, and settled near his father, about a mile south of the meeting house. He carried on the tailor's trade many years. He died Jan. 1, 1860, aged 85. Mrs. Wright is still alive. This couple sustained the marriage relation for sixty-four years. Their children were six in number:—Luther, Roxanna, who married Joseph Marsh of Hadley, Sally, Theodore, Julia, who married Sidney S. Avery, Clarrissa, who married Rev. Charles Lord.

Luther graduated at Yale College in 1822, was for several years tutor in that college; then licensed to preach the gospel; was afterwards employed Associate Principal of a school in Ellington, Ct., and as Principal of Leicester Academy. In 1841, on the opening of Williston Seminary for the admission of students, he was called to the position of Principal, which he accepted. After his resignation of that position in 1849, he taught a private Classical School for several years. He still resides in this place. Great credit is due to him for his labors as Principal of Williston Seminary. By the thoroughness of his instruction and discipline, the school acquired under him a character which, in connection with its munificent endowment, speedily gave it a place among the first academical institutions of our country. Since his retirement from that position, he has been prominent among those whose efforts have been put forth in the interests of education in his native town.

In this connection it may not be out of place, without injustice to others, to mention E. A. Hubbard, for many years instructor in the mathematical and philosophical department of Williston Seminary, as another who has taken great interest in the cause of education, in our community, as well as elsewhere.

Some years since Mr. Wright delivered a very able address before the Young Men's Association of Easthampton, in regard to the early history of the town. This Historical Sketch was published, and from it, as well as from the semi-centennial sermon of Rev. Mr. Williston, we have derived essential aid.

Theodore L. entered Yale College, in 1825, but owing ill health, he remained not quite two years. In 1833 he received the honorary degree of A. M. from that college. For a time he was employed as Principal of the Hartford City Grammar School, but is now engaged in business in Wisconsin.

Elijah Wright, brother of Dea. Stephen, and son of him who first settled in the town, was born August 22, 1733, married Mary Strong, daughter of Ichabod Strong of Southampton, and lived on the farm which his father bought when he first moved his residence from Northampton. His family consisted of five daughters and four sons. His oldest daughter, Mary, married Benjamin Lyman; Hannah married Enos Janes; Esther married ——— Russell of Warwich; Eunice married Benoni Clark of Westhampton; Asenath married Jonathan Connable of Bernardston. His four sons, Elijah, Daniel, Medad, and Ichabod, lived in their native town. Daniel married and lived on his father's place. Elijah, the oldest son, born August 30, 1765, built a house on the same farm, the one now owned by his son Samuel. His employment was that of a tanner and shoemaker. His death occurred January 8, 1814. His wife was Naomi Kingsley, a native of Westhampton. She survived her husband forty-three years. Their children were two, Naomi, who married Col. Thomas Pomeroy of Northampton, and Samuel, who still resides on his father's place. In early life he taught considerable in Common Schools, and in later years was often a member of the General School Committee. Elijah H., his son, graduated at Amherst College in 1842, and studied medicine in Hanover, N. H., and at Charleston, S. C. He then settled in Marietta, Ga., where he acquired quite an extensive medical practice.

Ichabod, youngest son of Elijah, Sen., born August 24, 1776, removed to Park Hill, and occupied the house built by Josiah Phelps. He married Mary Clapp, daughter of Jonathan Clapp. He was a prominent member of the church, an active, working Christian, ever ready to stand in his lot and bear his part in the work of the church. Often the weekly neighborhood prayer meeting was held at his house, and when it was at the school-house, or elsewhere, he was almost always present, ready, by prayer and exhortation, to contribute to the interest and profit of the occasion. These neighborhood gatherings for social prayer and conference, were a source of great spiritual profit to those who attended them, and through them to the whole district, as well as to the church. His death occurred in 1844. His children were Horace, Ichabod Strong, Edmund, J. Rockwell, and Russell M. Horace owned and worked a tannery for a number of years, at Roberts Meadow, in Northampton; afterwards removed to Syracuse, N. Y., and now resides in St. Louis, Mo. I. Strong resides in Brooklyn. Edmund graduated at Williams College in 1836; studied theology at East Windsor, Ct.; was ordained minister of the gospel; labored as a home missionary for many years in Weston, Mo.; afterwards was pastor of a church in St. Louis, Mo., and has been Secretary of the Home Missionary Society in that State. He is a faithful laborer, and has been the means of great good to those for whom he has labored. J. Rockwell lived on the old homestead for many years, but finally sold it, and removed to South Hadley, where he now resides. Russell M. graduated at Williams College in 1841, and was one of the early and efficient teachers of Williston Seminary. He afterwards removed to Georgia, where he was employed as Principal of a female educational institution, located at Athens. On the breaking out of the war, he returned to his native place, and is now Instructor in Natural Sciences in Williston Seminary.

GENEALOGY OF THE JANES FAMILY.

This family originally came from Kirtling, in the county of Cambridge, England, where it had been seated in 1235, when William de Janes, in fulfillment of a vow, made a pilgrimage to the tomb of our Saviour at Jerusalem.

The coat of arms of the family is thus described:—Arms—Argent—a lion rampant—azure—between three escallop shells—gules—Crest--Out of a ducal coronet, gold, a demi-lion, rampant—azure—holding between the paws an escallop shell—gules.

The lion rampant in the arms, shows that the ancestor had won a battle, while in command of the forces engaged. The escallop shells show that he had made a pilgrimage to the Holy Land. The ducal coronet was given to those who held command in the armies of the sovereign duke of the French Confederation.

William Janes, a native of Cambridge, England, came to this country from Essex, and first established himself in New Haven, Conn., probably as early as 1638. In 1654 or 5, he came to Northampton, and in 1657 was chosen Recorder of Laws, which office he retained for twenty years. He also conducted religious services on the Sabbath. Two of his children, Ebenezer and Jonathan, were slain at Northfield, Sept. 2, 1675, when that town was attacked by the Indians. His daughter Ruth married the first John Searl of Northampton, whose son John, together with three children, were killed by the Indians at Pascommuck, at the time of the massacre there. Benjamin Janes, son of William, removed to Easthampton about the year 1700. His was one of the first five families who dwelt in Pascommuck. At the time of the massacre there, two of his children were put to death, and his wife was taken to the top of Pomeroy's mountain, scalped, and left for dead. She however, was found, and taken to Northampton, where she recovered. She lived afterwards until she was more than eighty years old. Mr. Janes subsequently went to Coventry, Conn., probably in company with "a number of respectable persons from Northampton," who went about that time.

Samuel Janes, another son of William, married Sarah Hinsdale of Deerfield, daughter of Samuel Hinsdale, who was slain at Bloody Brook, in 1675. He also moved to

Easthampton, about 1700, and was one of the first five settlers in Pascommuck. In 1704, he, with his wife and three children, Obadiah, Ebenezer, and Sarah, were slain by the Indians. Samuel, his oldest son, then about eleven years of age, was taken prisoner. Just before the savages encountered Capt. John Taylor's troop of cavalry, they knocked him in the head and left him, doubtless supposing they had killed him. He however recovered from the effects of the blow, was one of those who re-settled his native village, and was the ancestor of all the persons bearing the name of Janes in this town, besides a numerous posterity in other parts of the country. His daughter Rachel married Capt. Philip Clark. He had four sons, all of whom settled in Easthampton. Their names were Samuel, Jonathan, Obadiah, Elisha.

In early life, Obadiah Janes was a teacher of common schools. In 1788 he was chosen deacon of the church, which office he held nineteen years. His wife was Beulah Lyman, daughter of Abner Lyman of Northampton, to whom he was much attached. She was a woman of strong mind and ardent piety. This couple sustained the marriage relation during the long period of fifty-seven years. Of them it might be said "they were lovely and pleasant in their lives and in death they were not divided" Both died in 1817, in the eighty-eighth year of their life. His death occurred first, but his wife survived only about two weeks. He lived on the place now occupied by Elisha Parsons, almost within a stone's throw of Connecticut river, yet it is said that he never crossed it. They were not blessed with children, but were blessed with large hearts, and consequently became "Uncle and Aunt" to no small portion of the community. Many persons now living, no doubt recall with pleasure, the hours spent in their younger days, beneath the hospitable roof of "Uncle Diah and Aunt Beulah."

In the same house with him, lived his brother Elisha. He had three daughters: Sarah, who married Asahel Parsons; Rachel, who married Joel Parsons; Mercy, who married Capt. Thaddeus Parsons.

Jonathan Janes, son of Samuel, settled where Waldo Prouty now resides. He was present at the surrender of Louisburg to the British and American forces, July 26, 1758. He died in 1825, being the oldest person who ever lived in this town. His age was ninety-nine years. He had a great propensity for story telling, and was, withal, quite witty. The following, related of him, will serve as an illustration. On one occasion, a wild steer belonging to him, escaped from his enclosure, and, upon search being made, was found upon the summit of Mt. Tom. Those who were in search of him, attempted to drive him, but the animal, actuated by fear, probably, leaped from a ledge, and was killed. Mr. Janes, afterwards, in relating the circumstance to some one, concluded by saying, "It most ruined his hide." He had three daughters: Esther; Lois, who married Dea. Solomon Lyman; and Rebekah, who married Daniel Wright. Of his four sons, Ebenezer, Jonathan, Parsons, Obadiah, the oldest moved to Napoli, N. Y., while the other three lived in Easthampton.

Jonathan, born Jan. 1, 1771, married Rachel, daughter of Capt. Philip Clark, and moved to the center of the town, where he built the house in which his grandson, Edwin S. Janes, now lives. His children were Lowell E., who resides in Easthampton; Rachel married Ezekiel White; Jonathan, who died in early life; Jason, whose home is in Brecksville, Ohio; two daughters, who died young; Spencer, who lived on his father's farm. He died in September, 1854, and his place is now occupied by his son, Edwin S. Janes.

Obadiah Janes married Esther, daughter of Lemuel Lyman, and afterwards Mary Chapman, daughter of David Chapman. He kept store near the hotel, where Ebenezer Ferry formerly lived, and where he for a time kept store. He had eleven children, none of whom settled in East-hampton. Of these, Esther, married Coleman Clark. Theodore learned the trade of book-binding and settled in Boston. Hamilton and Ellsworth now reside in Princeton, Ill., the former a farmor, and the latter a photographer. Lyman lived in Hadley. Francis and Justus entered the ministry.

Francis graduated at Williams, in 1830; studied theology at Auburn, N. Y., and labored in several different places in Central New York. He was last at Colchester, where he died Jan. 20, 1855.

In speaking of him the *Independent* said: "In every church where he has labored, God has blessed his instrumentality with precious revivals, and as the fruits of these revivals, about 300 have been gathered into the churches under his care. He was noted for his ardent piety, implicit faith, and a heart full of Christian sympathy and knowledge. He was a man full of faith and the Holy Spirit. During his whole ministry he lost not a Sabbath or a day from sickness."

To this very faithful notice of him, it may be added, that his early advantages for gaining knowledge were limited, and, moreover, he was naturally rather slow in its acquirement. He was dependent upon his own exertions for funds to support him in his collegiate course, and had it not been for his indomitable energy, and untiring perseverance, strengthened by a warm-hearted Christian zeal, he would have yielded to the seemingly insurmountable obstacles that opposed him, and relinquished the idea of acquiring an education. Had he done so, the ministry would have been deprived of one of its brightest ornaments.

15*

Justus Janes, brother of Francis, graduated at Amherst College; studied theology, and labored many years in various places in New York. He is now pastor of the Presbyterian Church in Chester, Ohio. He has been a man of extensive usefulness, beloved by all who have known him.

Parsons Janes, another of the four brothers last referred to, married Dorcas, daughter of Elam Clark, and settled on his father's farm. His family consisted of eight daughters and one son, all of whom married, and lived in Easthampton. Edwin, the son, married Catherine Wright; Dorcas was the wife of Joel Parsons; Triphenia, wife of Wm. N. Clapp; Julia, wife of C. Edson Wait; Lois, wife of Horace Clark; Martha, wife of Chester Wait; Harriet, wife of C. Edson Wait; Emily, wife of William N. Clapp; Elvira, wife of Waldo Prouty.

Samuel Janes, the other son of Samuel, married Hannah Brown, and settled on the place now occupied by Alanson Clark. His family consisted of five sons and two daughters, viz: Noah, Samuel, Enos, Asahel, Seth, Hannah, Sarah.

Seth lived for many years on the old place, with whom his brother Asahel remained, but in the latter part of his life, he moved to the center of the town, to the place now owned by Horace Matthews.

Enos settled on the farm where his son Luke now resides. His children were Nancy, who married and removed to the west; Lovisa, wife of David Montague of Westhampton; Helena, wife of Dwight Lyman; Luke; Samuel, who lives in Westhampton.

Capt. Noah Janes lived on the place afterwards owned by Asa Ferry. He took great interest in the affairs of the town, in which he was often engaged. After his family were grown up, he removed to Vermont. His children were Noah, Chester, Sylvanus, Lucas, Julius, Lewis, Patty, Electa, Naomi. The only descendants of this family who at present reside in town are those of the last named daughter, who married Sylvester Lyman.

WILLISTON.

Rev. Payson Williston was in the fourth generation from Joseph Williston, who lived in Westfield in 1691. He traded some with the Indians, and, as this trade was forbidden to all who were not licensed, his skins and furs were seized by Porter Tilton of Hadley, one of the magistrates. The case was carried to the county court. He pleaded ignorance of the law, and the court ordered the property to be restored to him. A few years after this he lived at Springfield, where he married Mrs. Mary Ashley, who was a daughter of Joseph Parsons, one of the first settlers of Northampton.

The children of Rev. Payson Williston, were Nathan Birdseye, who died at the age of four years; Maria, who married Theodore Brackett; Samuel; Nathan Birdseye, who is engaged in the mercantile business in Brattleboro; Sally, who married Josiah D. Whitney of Northampton. John Payson married Clarrissa, daughter of Asahel Lyman, resides in Northampton, and has been distinguished as an ardent friend and supporter of the temperance and anti-slavery causes.

The oldest son, Samuel, was born before the place was incorporated as a town, and has always resided here. In early life he entered upon a course of study preparatory for college, at Philips Academy, in Andover, the hope of his father being that he might be led to dedicate himself to God, and that then he might devote himself to the work of the ministry. He was finally compelled by weakness of eyes to relinquish his plans of study, and the trial thus sent upon him God was pleased to use as an instrument in bringing him to surrender himself into His hands. Then it was his great desire to prepare for the work of the ministry if it should be God's will. It was His design, however, that he should serve the cause of Christ in another field of labor. There were institutions of learning to be established and sustained, from which were to go forth many faithful ministers of the Cross, and some one must be raised up with the heart and the means for this work. Time has revealed that Mr. Williston was an instrument chosen of God for this purpose; and therefore he has labored more effectively than if he had been suffered to pursue his original intention.

By the frugality and industry which must be exercised in a country parsonage, he acquired those habits of life which admirably fitted him, under God, to achieve success in the business in which he engaged. It is needless, in this connection, to add to what we have already said of his remarkable success, especially in manufacturing. It is to the business which he has inaugurated and largely conducted, that the town owes its present position, as one of the largest towns in the county and the most rapidly growing. Many other men in various callings, it is true, have contributed to this growth and prosperity, but he must be recognized as the leading agent in it. The property which God has thus given him he has liberally bestowed in behalf of the cause of education.

It was at the darkest hour of the history of Amherst college, when the debt was rapidly increasing and there were no funds to procure such improvements as a growing institution required for its success, that Mr. Williston came to its aid. He endowed two professorships and the half of another, thus making a donation of $50,000. This relieved the college from its embarrassment, and gave it an increased power in the community. After the burning of North college, he erected on its site the building which bears his name, and which contains the chemical laboratory, together with the alumni and society halls.

But his largest benefactions have been to Williston Seminary, on which he has expended, or will soon have done so, the sum of $225,000, besides in the aggregate a large amount of time and labor.

In 1840 he served as a Representative, and in the two following years as a Senator in the state legislature.

The Payson church, twice re-built after being twice destroyed by fire, together with the rebuilding of the adjoining parsonage, after the second fire, has cost him the sum of $43,000, not including the sum expended in repairing the damage done by the blowing over of the steeple.

"About the year 1854, he engaged in the almost hopeless enterprise of building the Hampshire and Hampden railroad, thus extending the Canal railroad, and connecting Northampton with New Haven, through his own town. This he finally succeeded in accomplishing, after many delays and amid ceaseless opposition in the Legislature from the friends of other roads, having been elected president, and having sunk $35,000 for the public good." For a number of years he was president of the Holyoke Bank, and he has held that position in the First National Bank of Easthampton ever since its establishment.

Undoubtedly these facts are known to many of those who will read this sketch, yet it is but fitting that they should find a place in the history of the town to whose progress he has so largely contributed.

KNIGHT.

Roswell and Sylvester Knight, who were the first persons of that name residing here, removed from Huntington, in the early part of the present century. The former was a clothier by trade. He married Margaret, daughter of Jonathan Clapp. Their children were, Albert, Franklin, Artemas, Daniel, Henry, Margaret and Mary, none of whom now reside here.

Sylvester married Rachel, daughter of Capt. David Lyman, for his second wife, and lived where S. M. Lyman now does. The children of the second marriage were Rachel; Alice, wife of Isaac K. Clapp; Lothrop; Horatio G.; Sarah.

Sylvester, an older son, resides in Southampton.

Horatio G. began his career as a manufacturer about the time of the transferance of the button works from Haydenville, in 1847. He had before been connected with the business of Mr. Williston, as clerk and salesman; but about this time he became a partner in the concern. Since then, the button works have been carried on, as has elsewhere been said, by the firm of Williston, Knight & Co., until the recent organization of the National Button Co., in which the same persons are stockholders. Mr. Knight is also largely interested in the Nashawannuck and Glendale Companies, and next to Mr. Williston has been most prominent in the manufacturing operations of the place.

He has also been very prominent in the public affairs of the town, which he has twice represented in the Lower House of the Legislature. He also occupied a seat in the Senate during two sessions, and was a member of the Republican National Convention at Chicago, by which Abraham Lincoln was first placed before the people as a candidate for the Presidency.

In the early part of the war Mr. Knight was very active, procuring volunteers, paying bounties to Easthampton men who enlisted in the 27th regiment, and subsequently to those who enlisted in the 31st regiment, amounting in the aggregate to several thousand dollars.

In addition to the two already spoken of, and who are natives of the town, Seth Warner and Edmund H. Sawyer may be mentioned as identified with the manufacturing interests of the place. Mr. Warner has been a partner in the firm of Williston, Knight & Co., since its organization, and is now connected with the Rubber Thread Co., as its agent. The principal interest of Mr. Sawyer has been with the Nashawannuck Co., to whose efficient labors no small share of its success is due. He is now largely interested in the Glendale Co. Both these gentlemen have contributed much to the prosperity of the place since their removal hither.

PARSONS.

As it respects the origin of this name, some have supposed that it was derived from the word "parson," a clerical title given, from the fact that a clergyman is the principal person in a church. Hence in law he is termed *ecclesiæ personæ*, and has full possession of all the rights of a parrochial church. The s is added for the sake of euphony, or from the fact that the person to whom it was applied was the parson's son. Others have derived it from the word "parish," meaning son of the parish, or one supported by the parish. Still others have supposed that the name is the same with Peerson, Pierson and Pearson, modified in the spelling. These last are derived, according to Camden, from "son of Peter" or "Peterson." The family of Parsons was an ancient one in England. Sir Thomas Parsons of Milton Royal in England, about the year 1634, received the honor of knighthood from King Charles I. Cornet Joseph Parsons, who came from England, was one of the first settlers of Northampton, and owned a large tract of land in Pascommuck. His fourth son, Ebenezer, who was killed by the Indians at Northfield, was the first white child born in Northampton.

In the fifth generation from Cornet Joseph, was Dea. Joel Parsons, who removed to Easthampton. He was often employed when a young man, as teacher of the early district schools of the town. He was chosen deacon of the church in 1798, to fill the vacancy caused by the death of Benjamin Lyman.

He had five sons, all of whom lived in Easthampton. Aaron lived in his father's place, where his son Joseph now lives. Ebenezer Ferry lived where the house of E. R. Bosworth now stands. His trade was that of a blacksmith. Senaah married Lois, daughter of Solomon Lyman, and lived on the same place with his brother Aaron. He had but one child, L. Watson, who lives on a place adjoining that of his father. Joel was a joiner by trade, built and lived in the house owned by the late Lewis Ferry. He is said to have made the first sleigh which was driven in Easthampton. His wife was Rachel Janes. Their children were, Dixelana, married Bela Clark; Rachel married James Phelps; Climena married Wm. Gillett, and after his death became the second wife of Bela Clark; Angeline married Rev. Norris Day; Ann Frances married Lysander White, and afterwards Edson White; Ralph, Joel, Elisha, Luman, Frederick, Henry, George. Of the sons only one, Joel, remained in his native town. Ralph lives in Holyoke, and the four last named engaged in business elsewhere.

Thaddeus, son of Dea. Joel, lived in Pascommuck. He was for a long time connected with the military company of the town, and was for a number of years its captain. He was lieutenant of the company sent from South and Easthampton, to the defence of Boston, in the year 1812. His children were Mercy, who died in youth; Thaddeus K.; and Elisha, who now lives where his father did.

Edmund Parsons, who is an inhabitant of the east part

of the town, is a great-grandson of John Parsons, who lived in Northampton, and was in the fourth generation from Cornet Joseph. John was uncle to Dea. Joel, who has been mentioned.

Levi Parsons, a native of Goshen, removed to Easthampton soon after the establishment of the button works of Williston, Knight & Co., and was employed as their superintendent. Since that time he has been very intimately connected with the business and public interests of the town, and has been very highly esteemed as a citizen. His recent death, which occurred while on a visit to the South on account of his health, occasioned a great loss both to the community and to the church.

FERRY.

Ebenezer Ferry, a grandson of Charles Ferry of Springfield, settled in Pascommuck probably about the year 1730, on the farm of Moses Hutchinson, who with one child, was slain by the Indians in 1704. His son, Lieut. Solomon, succeeded him, and died here in the year 1810, aged 66. The name of his wife was Hannah French. To them were born the following children:—Polly, who married Seth Janes; Solomon; Asa; Ebenezer, who died at the age of twenty-five; Lovisa and Hannah, who died in childhood; Hannah, who married John Alpress.

Asa married Eunice Clark, and settled in the western portion of Pascommuck. Their children were Juliana, who married Luther Clark; Sidney, who lived on his father's farm; Lovisa married Ithamar Clark; Robert and Asa died in infancy; Eunice S. married Daniel F. Lyman; Ruth C. married Josiah Gaylord of South Hadley; Robert S. resides in Springfield; Adaline married E. Hazen of Springfield.

Solomon lived for many years on his father's farm, which was that now owned by Dea. E. Alonzo Clark. His first wife was Parnel Chapin, of West Springfield. They had five children. Hiram was a printer by trade, and published the "Oracle," and afterwards the "Democrat," at Northampton, where he died in 1860. He was for a number of years connected with the Boston Custom House. Nelson removed to Corunna, Mich., where he died in 1846. Ebenezer remained in his native place, was for many years postmaster and storekeeper, and has served the town with fidelity in many offices. S. Chapin resides in Chester, O. Lewis published papers in Ohio, and also in Northampton; but spent the later portion of his life in his native town, where he died in 1865. Two children were born to Solomon by a second wife, Sophia L. Hastings. They were P. Sophia, who married William Strong of Northampton; and Julia Ann, who married Fred A. Spencer of Westfield.

WHITE.

Nathaniel White, who resided in the south part of this town was in the sixth generation from Elder John White, who came from England, probably from Chelmsford, in 1632, and settled in Cambridge, where he was a member of the first board of selectmen. About 1636, he went to Hartford, from which place, in 1659, he removed to Hadley, where he was one of the committee to lay out the town, and one of those appointed to manage the affairs of the plantation. In 1672, he returned to Hartford, where he died in the winter of 1683–4. Nathaniel, before mentioned, was born in South Hadley, Nov. 28, 1749, removed to Easthampton, and married Huldah, daughter of Eliakim Clark. Their children were Levi, Huldah, Clark, Jemima, Nathaniel, Theodosia, wife of John Hannum, and Ezekiel. The oldest, Levi, married Miriam Alvord, of South Hadley, and settled in Easthampton on his father's place. Of their children, Julius moved to Southampton;

Edson and Lysander settled in their native town; Lucena married Julius Pomeroy; Amanda married Augustine Munson.

Ezekiel, son of Nathaniel, lived on the farm now occupied by Daniel Rust 2d. He was a painter by trade; but spent a large amount of time in antiquarian researches. These he carried, probably, to a greater extent than any other man in this section, excepting Sylvester Judd of Northampton. In regard to this subject, they both felt, what has been expressed by another, that "It is an act of duty, and a just tribute of affection to the memory of our ancestors, to rescue, if possible, their names from the perishing records of time, and not only to incorporate them with the annals of the present, but, as objects of affectionate remembrance, inscribe them in our family memorials."

It is fitting that the author of these sketches should here acknowledge the aid which he has received in collecting many of the facts given in the genealogical record, from the papers of Mr. White, to which he had access.

CHAPMAN.

David Chapman, Sen., was born in the city of Norwich Conn., removed to this place in 1772, where he remained during the revolutionary war, after which he lived in South and Westhampton. He died in 1814.

In the year 1774, he bought of the town of Northampton, "a piece of common land, the estate of the inhabitants of said town, and which was formerly part of the county road leading from Northampton to Westfield." From the description in the deed of the land purchased, it appears that it was that on which the High School building, and the First Congregational Church and its parsonage now stand. The purchase price was $1.91 an acre, a price which seems small indeed when compared with its present value. He erected a dwelling where E. R. Bosworth now lives. Mr. Chapman himself, four of his sons, and at least seven of his grandsons, were blacksmiths. So entirely did this seem to be a family occupation, that many persons in childhood regarded the name of Chapman and blacksmith as synonymous. Two only of the sons, Moses and David, settled in Easthampton. One, Willet, was a soldier, and died at West Point, in the eighteenth year of his age.

David Chapman, Jr., born March 23, 1761, married Mary, daughter of Dea. Benjamin Lyman. He built a house where the parsonage now stands. He afterwards removed to the north side of the Manhan River, near Dennis Lyman's present residence, and carried on the blacksmith business in a shop which stood on the bank of the river. He had seven children: Mary, second wife of Obadiah Janes; Sophia, wife of John Clapp; Martha, David, Charles, George, Moses, who all followed the occupation of their father, though Moses alone remained in town. He lived where Dr. Winslow now does. His shop stood near the present location of the Town Hall. His sons, Moses and John went West. Another son, Almon, for many years followed the ancestral employment, who, on his retirement, was in turn succeeded by his son, Almon S. Thus it will be seen that, as one family of Clapps were, through successive generations, the tavern keepers and millers of the town, so the Chapman family may be said to have been the blacksmiths.

POMEROY.

Eltweed Pomeroy, who came from Devonshire, England, to this country in 1630, lived at Dorchester and Windsor, and died in Northampton in 1673, and was the progenitor of a large portion if not of all who bear that name in the

United States. He is represented to have been a man of good family, tracing his pedigree back to Sir Ralph de Pomeroy, a favorite knight of William the Conqueror, whom he accompanied into England, acting a conspicuous part in the battle of Hastings, fought Oct. 14, 1066, and afterwards building a castle, called Berry Pomeroy, still in preservation on the grant which he received from the crown.

In the third generation from Eltweed were Samuel and Eldad Pomeroy, who settled in Easthampton about 1732, the latter near where John M. Clapp lives, and the former opposite, on land owned by Dea. E. W. Hannum. Soon after, Caleb, a son of Samuel, built a house on the hill west of his father's house, near the present residence of A. L. Strong. Of his children, Enos lived on his father's place, and Solomon where Eldad first established himself. Warham, son of Enos, succeeded his father, and had a large family of children, only one of whom, Hiram, is at present resident in town.

Of the children of Solomon, only one, who bore his father's name, remained in the town. He had but one child, Emeline, who married A. L. Strong.

Dea. Justus Pomeroy, who belonged to another branch of the family, was born in 1767, and settled in the western part of Easthampton near what was formerly known as "Pogue's Hole." By a recent change of town lines, the farm which he owned is now included within the limits of Southampton. He had five children: Spencer, who was mentioned as having performed service in the war of 1812; Jerusha, who married Joseph Haskins of Northampton; Triphenia, Julius, and Thomas Jefferson. The last three of these now reside in Easthampton.

Luther Pomeroy, who belonged to still another branch of the family, came to this town from Southampton and settled in the west part of the town, where his son Luther now lives. He also was mentioned as one of those who performed service in the war of 1812.

HANNUM.

William Hannum was one of the first proprietors of Northampton in 1653, and died there in 1677. In the fifth generation from him, were three brothers, early inhabitants of the town.

Sergt. Eleazer and John settled in the town, as early as 1760. Each of them had a son bearing their names, who succeeded to their property, and who were the fathers of the present owners of the estates. Eleazer W., who was chosen deacon of the church in 1833, and still holds the office, is the grandson of the former and owns his place; and John M. and Edwin are grandsons of the latter, and own his place. The second John Hannum bore the office of selectman for twenty years, a longer period than it has been held by any other man.

Joel, another of the brothers mentioned, settled in Nashawannuck. His sons, Paul and Julius, shared the ownership of his farm after his death, and each had large families. They, however, removed to the west many years since, and the only members of these families at present residing here are Arlow and Lucas W., sons of the former. Esther, daughter of Joel, married Simeon Clark; Phebe, married Oliver Clark; Jerusha, married Elijah Gloyd; Diana, married and now lives in Washington.

PHELPS.

"Ould Mr. Wm. Phelps, Esq. came from England to this country in 1630; was representative from Dorchester to the first court in 1634; removed to Windsor, Ct. in 1635; and was a member of the first court in that colony in 1636. He was a member of the General Court twelve sessions; and one of the most efficient and valuable officers in the colony." In the sixth generation from him, was William Phelps, who lived in the north part of this town, in a house which stood a short distance west of the road leading to Northampton. His son, Elijah, succeeded him, of whose children only Samuel remains here. Capt. John Phelps, father of James and Frederick, who live in the same district, removed thither from Northampton.

LUDDEN.

Lieut. Ezra Ludden removed from Braintree to Williamsburg in 1773, and thence to this place in 1779. He was a great reader, and took a great interest in the Library association, of which he was an active member. He died here in November, 1833, aged 86.

Of his sons, only one, John, remained in town. He was very prominent in public affairs; was the second person appointed Justice of the Peace; was selectman during a period of 18 years; and several times represented the town in the Legislature.

WOOD.

Ezekiel Wood was the first person bearing the name of Wood who lived in Easthampton. He was connected with the army in the war of the Revolution as Surgeon, and died at West Point while in the service. He had seven children, viz.: Daniel, David, Seth, Ezekiel, Stephen, Polly, Tamasind.

Daniel and David were also soldiers in the Revolutionary war. David afterwards settled in Southampton. Daniel moved to Palmyra, N. Y., where he died in the 98th year of his age. The following notice of him was published at the time of his death:—"He entered the service in early life, and was one of those hardy veterans who penetrated the wilderness to Quebec with Col. Arnold in April, 1775. He remained before Quebec through the following winter. He was also one of the soldiers at Saratoga, and served through the war."

Tamasind was the wife of Thaddeus Clark. Ezekiel was shot accidentally by one of his neighbors while they were hunting deer. Seth lived for a time in Easthampton, and was the father of E. T. Wood, who now resides in Northampton. Stephen married Jemima, daughter of Obadiah Clark, by whom he had four children, Gaius, Stephen, Jemima, and Mary. He afterwards married Sally Braman. Their children were Ezekiel, Enoch E., Newton, S. Chapin, and Sarah. These last mentioned all live in this town, excepting Ezekiel, who died here recently.

HENDRICK.

Israel Hendrick was the first settler in the south-east part of the town, whither he removed about the year 1774, and built a log house on the east side of Broad Brook. He had three sons, viz.: Reuben, who removed to Conway, had several children, and died about the year 1800, at the age of 55 years. Moses, who settled in Hoosick, N. Y., acquired considerable property and died in 1845, at the advanced age of 100 years. James, the youngest son, removed to the opposite side of the brook from where his father lived, and built the house now occupied by Pearson Hendrick. He had eleven children, eight sons and three daughters. Jesse, the oldest, died at the age of twenty-four; Pearson died in early childhood; Huldah, James, Lovy, Reuben, Joseph, Stephen, Pearson, Jabez, and Rachel. Five of the above brothers settled in this neighborhood, and four of them are still alive and reside within half a mile of each other. The youngest son, Jabez settled elsewhere.

APPENDIX.

A few typographical errors and omissions escaped notice in the correction of the proof, which should be inserted here. If others still exist, we crave the reader's indulgence.

On page 9 instead of John Scott read George Frary.

On page 147 read Alender instead of Aleander.

On page 148 instead of 1830 read 1835.

In our notice of the Internal Revenue, we should have mentioned the fact that George S. Clark was the immediate successor of Levi Parsons as Assistant Assessor, which office he held a few months when he was succeeded by Lafayette Clapp.

COLLEGE GRADUATES.

The following list of the natives of the town who have received college honors, will be interesting as a matter of reference:—

Azariah Clark,	Class	of	1805,	Williams	College.
Job Clark,	"	"	1811,	"	"
Elam C. Clark,	"	"	1812,	"	"
Theodore Clapp,	"	"	1814,	Yale	"
Solomon Lyman,	"	"	1822,	"	"
Sumner G. Clapp,	"	"	1822,	"	"
Luther Wright,	"	"	1822,	"	"
Sylvester Clapp,	"	"	1823,	Union	"
Silas C. Brown,	"	"	1828,	"	"
Theodore L. Wright,	"	"	1829,	Yale	"
Samuel Matthews,	"	"	1829,	Amherst	"
Francis Janes,	"	"	1830,	Williams	"
Thornton W. Clapp,	"	"	1835,	"	"
Edmund Wright,	"	"	1836,	"	"
Josiah Lyman,	"	"	1836,	"	"
Alender O. Clapp,	"	"	1837,	Amherst	"

Addison Lyman,	Class of 1839,	Williams College
Jabez B. Lyman,	" " 1841,	Amherst "
Russell M. Wright,	" " 1841,	Williams "
Horace Lyman,	" " 1842,	" "
Elijah H. Wright,	" " 1842,	Amherst "
William S. Clark,	" " 1848,	" "
Lyman R. Williston,	" " 1850,	" "
Edson L. Clark,	" " 1853,	Yale "
Francis H. Hannum,	" " 1865,	Amherst "
James T. Graves,	" " 1866,	Yale "
Payson W. Lyman,	" " 1867,	Amherst "

Nearly all of these have been noticed particularly in the Genealogical Record. Of those not thus alluded to, Sylvester Clapp studied Theology and was ordained and settled in Maine.

Silas C. Brown studied Theology, and was ordained and settled in the ministry in the state of New York.

Samuel Matthews became President of Hampden Sidney College. He died in 1853, at the age of 51.

William S. Clark, after his graduation at Amherst, was employed as teacher in Williston Seminary, then studied in a German University, and has since held the Professorship of Chemistry in Amherst College.

Lyman R. Williston taught in Williston Seminary for a time after his graduation, then studied theology in Andover, after which he went to Germany, and studied in Berlin. On his return he was employed as Principal of the Cambridge High School. He is now teaching a private school in Cambridge.

It will be seen by reference to this list that the number of men from the town obtaining a collegiate education has decreased within the last twenty years, about as fast as the town has increased in population, a fact which it would seem ought not so to be.

www.ingramcontent.com/pod-product-compliance
Lightning Source LLC
LaVergne TN
LVHW011219110826
845150LV00006B/1473
* 9 7 8 1 4 2 5 5 1 5 9 4 2 *